Cultural Differences in Educational Leadership

Cultural Differences in Educational Leadership

Lessons from Heaven's Messengers, Melting Pot or Not!

Robert Palestini

ROWMAN & LITTLEFIELD
Lanham • Boulder • New York • London

Published by Rowman & Littlefield
A wholly owned subsidiary of The Rowman & Littlefield Publishing Group, Inc.
4501 Forbes Boulevard, Suite 200, Lanham, Maryland 20706
www.rowman.com

Unit A, Whitacre Mews, 26-34 Stannary Street, London SE11 4AB

Copyright © 2016 by Robert Palestini

All rights reserved. No part of this book may be reproduced in any form or by any electronic or mechanical means, including information storage and retrieval systems, without written permission from the publisher, except by a reviewer who may quote passages in a review.

British Library Cataloguing in Publication Information Available

Library of Congress Cataloging-in-Publication Data

Names: Palestini, Robert H., author
Title: Cultural differences in educational leadership : lessons from heaven's messengers, melting pot or not! / Robert Palestini.
Description: Lanham, Maryland : Rowman & Littlefield, 2016. | Includes bibliographical references.
Identifiers: LCCN 2016023173 (print) | LCCN 2016036437 (ebook) | ISBN 9781475827279 (cloth : alk. paper) | ISBN 9781475827286 (pbk. : alk. paper) | ISBN 9781475827309 (Electronic)
Subjects: LCSH: Educational leadership--Philosophy. | Educational leadership--Cross-cultural studies. | Education--Religious aspects.
Classification: LCC LB2805 .P2875 2016 (print) | LCC LB2805 (ebook) | DDC 371.2/011--dc23
LC record available at https://lccn.loc.gov/2016023173

∞ ™ The paper used in this publication meets the minimum requirements of American National Standard for Information Sciences Permanence of Paper for Printed Library Materials, ANSI/NISO Z39.48-1992.

Printed in the United States of America

To Tom Koerner, whose longtime faith in me
as an author is much appreciated.

To Carlie Wall, for her invaluable contributions.

To Judy, whose support and encouragement mean the world to me.

To Karen, Scott, Rob, and Brendan,
whose presence in my life is rejuvenating.

To Liz, for willingly providing much-needed
clerical and technical assistance.

Contents

Introduction ... ix

1. Contemporary Leadership Theory ... 1
2. Leading with Heart ... 13
3. Moses ... 31
4. Gautama Buddha ... 37
5. Confucius ... 45
6. Jesus Christ ... 55
7. Muhammad ... 75
8. Mahatma Gandhi ... 85
9. Martin Luther King Jr. ... 99
10. Pope St. John Paul II ... 113
11. St. Mother Teresa ... 127
12. Pope Francis I ... 135
13. What Have You Learned? ... 147

Diagnostics ... 161
References ... 173
About the Author ... 175

Introduction

I have noticed recently that there has been a dramatic increase in the number of international students who are attending America's colleges and universities and pursuing their careers in the field of education, specifically in educational leadership. Having had the pleasure of having some of these students in my graduate courses in educational leadership, I did some research, and with the exception of studies like those of Caroline Rook and Anupam Agrawal's (2013) working paper "Global Leaders East and West—Do All Global Leaders Lead in the Same Way?" and Robert J. House's (1999) article "How Cultural Factors Affect Leadership," found that there was somewhat of a dearth of research studies, journal articles, and/or books that compared, contrasted, and analyzed the leadership theories, ideologies, and styles of Eastern versus Western cultures. This book is intended to help fill this apparent gap in the literature.

Since it can be argued that spiritual and religious leaders have had the most lasting effect on world society and its various cultures and are often the ones who serve as the best examples of what effective leadership looks like, I decided to examine the leadership behavior or enactments of some the most recognized spiritual and religious leaders from the past and the present in both the East and the West to see whether their leadership enactments are consistent among the various cultures and how they might inform our own leadership behavior.

In this book, I explore the leadership behavior and styles of the following ten individuals in chronological order: Moses, Gautama Buddha, Confucius, Jesus Christ, Muhammad, Mahatma Gandhi, St. John Paul II, Martin Luther King Jr., St. Mother Teresa, and Pope Francis I. I assert that these leaders' considerable impact on our global society was primarily due to their ability to place some form of situational leadership theory into effective practice. In analyzing their leadership styles, I apply the Lee Bolman and Terrence Deal (1991) model of situational leadership theory, which posits four frames of leadership behavior: (1) structural, (2) human resource, (3) symbolic, and (4) political. I supplement Bolman and Deal's model with a fifth frame, which I call the moral frame. As a note, Bolman and Deal argue that effective and impactful leaders combine and balance their use of these frames, rather than dwelling almost exclusively on one frame to the virtual exclusion of the others.

Basically, then, this is a book about leadership. The conventional wisdom is that leaders are born, not made. I disagree! My experience and, more importantly, a large body of scholarly research indicate that leadership skills can be learned. Granted, some leaders will be superior to others because of genetics, but the basic leadership skills are learned behaviors and can be cultivated, enhanced, and honed.

In that regard, the first chapter of this book speaks to the so-called "science" of leadership, while the second chapter deals with the "art" of administration and leadership. One needs to lead with both mind (science) and heart (art) to be truly effective. The next ten chapters are analyses of the leadership behavior of ten spiritual and religious leaders from the present and the past, East and West, and are predicated on the belief that leadership skills can be learned. In the last chapter, I conclude by looking at the overall leadership behavior of these leaders to determine how their behavior might inform our own particular leadership styles.

The effective building blocks of quality leadership are the skills of communication, motivation, organizational development, management, and creativity. Mastering the theory and practice in these areas of study, which I call leading with *mind,* will produce high-quality leadership ability and, in turn, produce successful leaders; doing so with "heart" will result in not only highly effective leadership, but what author Chris Lowney calls *heroic leadership* (Lowney 2003).

There is another broadly held assumption about effective leadership and administration that I would dispute. Namely, that "nice guys (and gals) finish last." To be a successful leader, the belief goes, one needs to be firm, direct, even autocratic. Once again, scholarly research, as well as my own experience, indicates that no one singular leadership style is consistently effective in all situations and at all times. Both empirical and experiential studies indicate that effective leaders vary their styles depending on the situation. This *situational* approach is the underlying theme of this book. In the concluding chapter, I assert that truly effective leaders, no matter their culture and society, use both their minds and their hearts in the leadership process, and in doing so, nice guys and gals do oftentimes finish *first.*

Some forty years ago, when I was coaching high-school basketball, I attended a coaching clinic where the main clinicians were Dean Smith, then varsity basketball coach of North Carolina University, and Bobby Knight, then coach of Indiana University. Both coaches were successful then, and more than four decades later, they remain respected and revered.

In the morning session, Bobby Knight explained how *fear* was the most effective motivator in sports. If you want athletes to listen to and follow your instructions and want to be successful as a coach, you need to instill fear in them, Knight declared. In the afternoon session, Dean Smith explained how *love* is the most effective motivator in sports and in life. If you want to win and be successful, you must evoke love in your players.

You can understand my sense of confusion by the end of that clinic. Here were two of the most successful men in sports giving contradictory advice. As a young and impressionable coach, I was puzzled by these apparently mixed messages. Over the intervening years, I have often thought about that clinic and tried to make sense of what I had heard. After these many years, I have drawn two conclusions from this incident, both of which have had a significant impact on my philosophy of leadership and on this book.

The first conclusion has to do with the *situational* nature of leadership. Bobby Knight and Dean Smith impressed upon me the truism that there is no one singular leadership style that is effective at all times and in all situations; and, secondly, that despite reaping short-term success, the better style for ensuring continued success is one that inspires love, trust, and respect. Just as athletes become robotic and frightened of making mistakes when fear is the only motivator, so do employees who are too closely supervised by an autocratic manager. Initiative, creativity, and self-sufficiency are all stymied by the leader who instills fear in his or her subordinates. Thus, I arrived at my conclusion that effective school administration in particular and leadership in general begins with love, trust, and respect.

In addition to an emphasis on the nature of leadership, this book focuses on placing *theory* into practice. We cannot underestimate the value and importance of theory. Without theory we have no valid way of analyzing and correcting failed practice. Without a theoretical base, we oftentimes lead by trial and error, or by the proverbial "seat of your pants." On the other hand, knowledge of theory without the ability to place it into reflective practice is of no value and not characteristic of effective leadership. I suggest that leaders and aspiring leaders adopt one of the leadership theories described in this book and place it into reflective practice, modeled after the leadership behavior of some of the leaders highlighted here.

This book uses the case-study approach in order to facilitate placing theory into effective practice. Each chapter contains an extensive study of one of ten of the most successful leaders in world history. We will analyze each case and see how these leaders were able to place situational leadership theory into effective practice. I believe that the lessons learned will prove invaluable to leaders and aspiring leaders, whether they be a parent, teacher, school principal, superintendent, university administrator, or CEO, and whether they are dealing with people from the United States or from another country and/or culture.

This book also suggests an organizational development approach to producing effective leadership. Picture yourself standing in the middle of a dense forest. Suppose you were asked to describe the characteristics of the forest; what types of trees are growing in the forest; how many acres of trees are there; where are the trees thriving; where are they not? Faced with this proposition, most people would not know where to start and "would not be able to see the forest for the trees."

Newly appointed executives and administrators often have this same feeling of confusion when faced with the prospect of having to assume a leadership role in a complex organization like a school, a school system, a college or a company. Where does one start? An effective place to start would be to systematically examine the components that make up an organization. Such a system of organizational diagnosis and prescription will lead to a comprehensive and integrated analysis of the organization's strengths and weaknesses and point the way toward possible improvement.

Using the leadership behaviors found among the successful men and woman profiled here as a foundation, the final chapter of this book suggests such a sequential and systematic approach. In the appendix, there is a pair of diagnostic tools that I developed called the *Heart Smart Survey I* and *II* that assess the organizational health of an institution. Utilizing them effectively can produce useful and sometimes dramatic results (Palestini 2014).

Chapter One

Contemporary Leadership Theory

The effective functioning of social systems from the local PTA to the United States of America is assumed to be dependent on the quality of their leadership.

—Victor H. Vroom

Leadership is offered as a solution for most of the problems of organizations everywhere. Schools will work, we are told, if principals provide strong instructional and organizational leadership. Around the world, administrators and managers say that their organizations would thrive if only senior management provided strategy, vision, and real leadership. Though the call for "leadership" is universal, there is much less clarity about what the term means.

Historically, researchers in this field have searched for the one best leadership style that would be most effective. Current thought is that there is no one best style. Rather, a combination of styles depending on the situation the leader finds himself or herself in has been found to be more appropriate. To understand the evolution of leadership theory thought, we will take an historical approach and trace the progress of leadership theory, beginning with the trait perspective of leadership and moving to the more current contingency theories of leadership.

THE TRAIT THEORY

Trait theory suggests that we can evaluate leadership and propose ways of leading effectively by considering whether an individual possesses certain personality traits, social traits, and physical characteristics. Popular in the

1940s and 1950s, trait theory attempted to predict which individuals would successfully become leaders.

Trait theorists suggest that leaders differ from nonleaders in their drive, desire to lead, honesty and integrity, self-confidence, cognitive ability, and knowledge of the business they are in. Even the traits judged necessary for top, middle, and low-level management differed among leaders of different countries; for example, United States and British leaders valued resourcefulness; the Japanese, intuition; and the Dutch, imagination, but for lower and middle managers only (Kirkpatrick and Locke 1991).

Of course, trait theory begs the question, can we think of any individuals who are effective leaders, but who lack one or more of these characteristics? Chances are that we can. Skills and ability to implement the vision are necessary to transform traits into leadership behavior. Individual capability, which is a function of background, predispositions, preferences, cognitive complexity, human relations, and technical and conceptual skills also contribute.

The trait approach has more historical than practical interest to managers and administrators, even though recent research in transformational leadership has once again tied leadership effectiveness to leader traits. For example, some view the transformational perspective described later in this chapter as a natural evolution of the earlier trait perspective.

THE BEHAVIORAL PERSPECTIVE

The limitations in the ability of traits to predict effective leadership caused researchers during the 1950s to view a person's *behavior* rather than that individual's personal traits as a way of increasing leadership effectiveness. This view also paved the way for later situational theories.

The types of leadership behaviors investigated typically fell into two categories: production oriented (autocratic) and employee oriented (democratic). Production-oriented leadership, also called concern for production, initiating structure, or task-focused leadership, involves acting primarily to get the task done. An administrator who tells his or her department chair to do "everything you need to get the new curriculum developed on time for the start of school no matter what the personal consequences" demonstrates production-oriented leadership. So does an administrator who uses an autocratic style and fails to involve others in any aspect of decision making.

Employee-oriented leadership, also called concern for people or the collaborative approach, focuses on supporting the individual workers in their activities and involving the workers in decision making. A principal who shares decision making and demonstrates great concern for his or her teachers' satisfaction with their duties and commitment to their work has an employee-oriented leadership style (Stogdill and Coons 1957).

EARLY SITUATIONAL THEORIES

Contingency or situational models differ from the earlier trait and behavioral models in asserting that no single way of leading works in all situations. Rather, appropriate behavior depends on the circumstances at a given time. Effective managers diagnose the situation, identify the leadership style that will be most effective, and then determine whether they can implement the required style. Early situational research suggested that subordinate, supervisor, and task considerations affect the appropriate leadership style in a given situation. The precise aspects of each dimension that influence the most effective leadership style vary.

THEORY X AND THEORY Y

One of the older situational theories, McGregor's Theory X/Theory Y formulation, calls for a leadership style based on individuals' assumptions about other individuals, together with characteristics of the individual, the task, the organization, and environment. Although managers may have many styles, Theories X and Y managers have received the greatest attention.

Theory X managers assume that people are lazy, extrinsically motivated, and incapable of self-discipline or self-control, and that they want security and no responsibility in their jobs. Theory Y managers assume people do not inherently dislike work, are intrinsically motivated, exert self-control, and seek responsibility. A Theory X manager, because of his or her limited view of the world, has only one leadership style available, that is, autocratic. A Theory Y manager is situational in that he or she has a wide range of styles in his or her repertoire (McGregor 1961).

How can an administrator use McGregor's theory for ensuring leadership effectiveness? What prescription would McGregor offer for improving the situation? If an administrator had Theory X assumptions, he would suggest that the administrator change them and would facilitate this change by sending the administrator to a management-development program. If a manager had Theory Y assumptions, McGregor would advise a diagnosis of the situation to ensure that the selected style matched the administrator's assumptions and action tendencies, as well as the internal and external influences on the situation.

FREDERICK FIEDLER'S THEORY

While McGregor's theory provided a transition from behavioral to situational theories, Frederick Fiedler developed and tested the first leadership theory explicitly called a contingency or situational model. He argued that changing an individual's leadership style is quite difficult, but that organizations should put individuals in situations that fit with their style. Fiedler's theory suggests that managers can choose between two styles: task oriented and relationship oriented. Then the nature of leader-member relations, task structure, and position power of the leader influences whether a task-oriented or a relationship-oriented leadership style is more likely to be effective.

Leader-member relations refer to the extent to which the group trusts and respects the leader and will follow the leader's directions. Task structure describes the degree to which the task is clearly specified and defined or structured, as opposed to ambiguous or unstructured. Position power means the extent to which the leader has official power, that is, the potential or actual ability to influence others in a desired direction owing to the position he or she holds in the organization.

The style recommended as most effective for each combination of these three situational factors is based on the degree of control or influence the leader can exert in his or her leadership position.

Despite extensive research to support the theory, critics have questioned the reliability of the measurement of leadership style and the range and appropriateness of the three situational components. This theory, however, is particularly applicable for those who believe that individuals are born with a certain management style, rather than the management style being learned or flexible (Fiedler and Garcia 1987).

CONTEMPORARY SITUATIONAL LEADERSHIP

Current research suggests that the effect of leader behaviors on performance is altered by such intervening variables as the effort of subordinates, their ability to perform their jobs, the clarity of their job responsibilities, the organization of the work, the cooperation and cohesiveness of the group, the sufficiency of resources and support provided to the group, and the coordination of work group activities with those of other subunits.

Thus, leaders must respond to these and broader cultural differences in choosing an appropriate style. A leader-environment-follower interaction theory of leadership notes that effective leaders first analyze deficiencies in the follower's ability, motivation, role perception, and work environment that inhibit performance and then act to eliminate these deficiencies (Biggart and Hamilton 1987).

PATH-GOAL THEORY

According to path-goal theory, the leader attempts to influence subordinates' perceptions of goals and the path to achieve them. Leaders can then choose among four styles of leadership: directive, supportive, participative, and achievement oriented. In selecting a style, the leader acts to strengthen the expectancy, instrumentality, and valence of a situation, respectively, by providing better technology or training for the employees; reinforcing desired behaviors with pay, praise, or promotion; and ensuring that the employees value the rewards they receive (House 1977 and 1999).

Choosing a style requires a quality diagnosis of the situation to decide what leadership behaviors would be most effective in attaining the desired outcomes. The appropriate leadership style is influenced first by subordinates' characteristics, particularly the subordinates' abilities and the likelihood that the leader's behavior will cause subordinates' satisfaction now or in the future; and second by the environment, including the subordinates' tasks, the formal authority system, the primary work group, and organizational culture.

According to this theory, the appropriate style for an administrator depends on his or her subordinates' skills, knowledge, and abilities, as well as their attitudes toward the administrator. It also depends on the nature of the activities, the lines of authority in the organization, the integrity of their work group, and the task technology involved. The most desirable leadership style helps the individual achieve satisfaction, meet personal needs, and accomplish goals, while complementing the subordinates' abilities and the characteristics of the situation.

Application of the path-goal theory, then, requires first an assessment of the situation, particularly its participants and environment, and second, a determination of the most congruent leadership style. Even though the research about path-goal theory has yielded mixed results, it can provide a leader with help in selecting an effective leadership style.

THE HERSEY/BLANCHARD MODEL

In an attempt to integrate previous knowledge about leadership into a prescriptive model of leadership style, this theory cites the "readiness of followers," defined as their ability and willingness to accomplish a specific task, as the major contingency that influences appropriate leadership style (Hersey and Blanchard 1969, 1988). Follower readiness incorporates the follower's level of achievement motivation, ability and willingness to assume responsibility for his or her own behavior in accomplishing specific tasks, and education and experience relevant to the task. The model combines task and relationship behavior to yield four possible styles: telling, selling, participating, and delegating.

Leaders should use a telling style, and provide specific instructions and closely supervise performance, when followers are unable and unwilling or insecure. Leaders should use a selling style, and explain decisions and provide opportunity for clarification, when followers have moderate-to-low readiness. Using a participating style, where the leader shares ideas and helps facilitate decision making, should occur when followers have moderate-to-high readiness. Finally, leaders should use a delegating style, and give responsibility for decisions and implementation to followers, when followers are able, willing, and confident.

Although some researchers have questioned the conceptual clarity, validity, robustness, and utility of the model, as well as the instruments used to measure leadership style, others have supported the utility of the theory. For example, the Leadership Effectiveness and Description Scale (LEAD) and related instruments, developed by life cycle researchers to measure leadership style, are widely used in industrial training programs. This model can easily be adapted to educational administration as well as other types of leadership positions and be used analytically to understand leadership deficiencies and combine it with the path-goal model to prescribe the appropriate style for a variety of situations.

BOLMAN/DEAL REFRAMING APPROACH

Lee Bolman and Terrence Deal have developed a unique approach to situational leadership theory that analyzes leadership behavior through four frames of reference: structural, human resource, political, and symbolic. Each of the frames offers a different perspective on what leadership is and how it operates in organizations. Each can result in either effective or ineffective conceptions of leadership (Bolman and Deal 1991).

Structural leaders develop a new model of the relationship of structure, strategy, and environment for their organizations. They focus on implementation. The right answer helps only if it can be implemented. These leaders emphasize rationality, analysis, logic, fact, and data. They are likely to believe strongly in the importance of clear structure and well-developed management systems. A good leader is someone who thinks clearly, makes good decisions, has good analytic skills, and can design structures and systems that get the job done.

Structural leaders sometimes fail because they miscalculate the difficulty of putting their designs in place. They often underestimate the resistance that will be generated, and they take few steps to build a base of support for their innovations. In short, they are often undone by human resource, political, and symbolic considerations. Structural leaders do continually experiment, evaluate, and adapt, but because they fail to consider the entire environment in which they are situated, they sometimes are ineffective.

Human resource leaders believe in people and communicate that belief. They are passionate about "productivity through people." They demonstrate this faith in their words and actions and often build it into a philosophy or credo that is central to their vision of their organizations. They believe in the importance of coaching, participation, motivation, teamwork, and good interpersonal relations.

A good leader is a facilitator and participative manager who supports and empowers others. Human resource leaders are visible and accessible. Peters and Waterman popularized the notion of "management wandering around," the idea that managers need to get out of their offices and interact with workers and customers. Many educational administrators have adopted this aspect of management.

Effective human resource leaders empower, that is, they increase participation, provide support, share information, and move decision making as far down the organization as possible. Human resource leaders often like to refer to their employees as "partners" or "colleagues." They want to make it clear that employees have a stake in the organization's success and a right to be involved in making decisions. When they are ineffective, however, they are seen as naive or as weaklings and wimps.

Political leaders believe that managers and leaders live in a world of conflict and scarce resources. The central task of management is to mobilize the resources needed to advocate and fight for the unit's or the organization's goals and objectives. They emphasize the importance of building a power base: allies, networks, coalitions. A good leader is an advocate and negotiator and understands politics and is comfortable with conflict. Political leaders clarify what they want and what they can get. Political leaders are realists above all. They never let what they want cloud their judgment about what is possible. They assess the distribution of power and interests. Their primary goal can be described as making friends and influencing people.

The political leader needs to think carefully about the players, their interests, and their power; in other words, he or she must map the political terrain. Political leaders ask questions such as: Whose support do I need? How do I go about getting it? Who are my opponents? How much power do they have? What can I do to reduce the opposition? Is the battle winnable? However, if ineffective, these leaders are perceived as being untrustworthy and manipulative.

The symbolic frame provides still a fourth turn of the kaleidoscope of leadership. In this frame, the organization is seen as a stage, a theater in which every actor plays certain roles and attempts to communicate the right impressions to the right audiences. The main premise of this frame is that whenever reason and analysis fail to contain the dark forces of ambiguity, human beings erect symbols, myths, rituals, and ceremonies to bring order, meaning, and predictability out of chaos and confusion. They believe that the essential role of management is to provide inspiration. They rely on personal charisma and a flair for drama to get people excited and committed to the organizational mission.

A good leader is a prophet and visionary who uses symbols, tells stories, and frames experience in ways that give people hope and meaning. Transforming leaders are visionary leaders, and visionary leadership is invariably symbolic. Examination of symbolic leaders reveals that they follow a consistent set of practices and rules.

Transforming leaders use symbols to capture attention. When a colleague of mine became principal of a middle school in inner-city Philadelphia, she knew that she faced a substantial challenge. Her school had all the usual problems of urban public schools: decaying physical plant, lack of student discipline, racial tension, troubles with the teaching staff, low morale, and limited resources. The only good news was that the situation was so bad that almost any change would be an improvement.

In such a situation, symbolic leaders will try to do something visible, even dramatic, to let people know that changes are on the way. During the summer before she assumed her duties, she wrote a letter to every teacher to set up an individual meeting. She traveled to meet teachers wherever they wanted, driving two hours in one case. She asked teachers how they felt about the school and what changes they wanted.

She also felt that something needed to be done about the school building because nobody likes to work in a dumpy place. She decided that the front door and some of the worst classrooms had to be painted. She had few illusions about getting the bureaucracy of a big-city public-school system to provide painters, so she persuaded some of her family members to help her do the painting. When school opened, students and staff members immediately saw that things were going to be different, if only symbolically. Perhaps even more important, staff members received a subtle challenge to make a contribution themselves.

Each of the frames captures significant possibilities for leadership, but each is incomplete. In the early part of the century, leadership as a concept was rarely applied to management, and the implicit models of leadership were narrowly rational. In the 1960s and 1970s, human resource leadership became fashionable. The literature on organizational leadership stressed openness, sensitivity, and participation.

In recent years, symbolic leadership had moved to center stage, and the literature now offers advice on how to become a visionary leader with the power to transform organizational cultures. Organizations do need vision, but it is not their only need and not always their most important one. Leaders need to understand their own frame and its limits. Ideally, they will also learn to combine multiple frames into a more comprehensive and powerful style.

It is through the Bolman/Deal leadership model lens that we will examine and analyze the leadership enactments of the ten religious leaders profiled in this book. Before leaving our discussion of Bolman and Deal's approach, however, let us reinforce the point that balance needs to occur both *among* and *within* the frames. That is to say that in addition to utilizing all four frames, the effective leader needs to be careful not to behave to the extreme within any one frame. Striving for the Golden Mean is the goal.

TRANSFORMATIONAL LEADERSHIP

A charismatic or transformational leader uses charisma to inspire his or her followers and is an example who acts primarily in the symbolic frame of leadership outlined above. He or she talks to the followers about how essential their performance is, how confident he or she is in the followers, how exceptional the followers are, and how he or she expects the group's performance to exceed expectations. Among the spiritual and religious leaders profiled in this study, virtually all of them were found to be transformational leaders. Such leaders use dominance, self-confidence, a need for influence, and conviction of moral righteousness to increase their charisma and consequently their leadership effectiveness (House 1977).

A transformational leader changes an organization by recognizing an opportunity and developing a vision, communicating that vision to organizational members, building trust in the vision, and achieving the vision by motivating organizational members. The leader helps subordinates recognize the need for revitalizing the organization by developing a felt need for change, overcoming resistance to change, and avoiding quick-fix solutions to problems.

The charismatic leader can also change the composition of the team, alter management processes, and help organizational members reframe the way they perceive an organizational situation. The charismatic leader must empower others to help achieve the vision. Finally, the transformational leader must institutionalize the change by replacing old technical, political, cultural, and social networks with new ones. For example, the leader can identify key individuals and groups, develop a plan for obtaining their commitment, and institute a monitoring system for following the changes.

If an administrator wishes to make an innovative program acceptable to the faculty and the school community, for example, he or she should follow the above plan and identify influential individuals who would agree to champion the new program, develop a plan to gain support of others in the community through personnel contact or other means, and develop a monitoring system to assess the progress of the effort (Palestini 1999).

A transformational leader motivates subordinates to achieve beyond their original expectations by increasing their awareness about the importance of designated outcomes and ways of attaining them; by getting workers to go beyond their self-interest to that of the team, the school, the school system, and the larger society; by changing or expanding the individual's needs. Subordinates report that they work harder for such leaders. In addition, such leaders are judged higher in leadership potential by their subordinates as compared to the more common transactional leader.

One should be cognizant, however, of the negative side of charismatic leadership that may exist if the leader overemphasizes devotion to himself or herself, makes personal needs paramount, or uses highly effective communication skills to mislead or manipulate others. Such leaders may be so driven to achieve a vision that they ignore the costly implications of their goals.

The superintendent of schools who overexpands his or her jurisdiction in an effort to build an "empire," only to have the massive system turn into a bureaucratic nightmare, is an example of transformational leadership gone sour. A business that expands too rapidly to satisfy the ego of the CEO, and as a result loses its handle on quality control is another example. Nevertheless, recent research has verified the overall effectiveness of the transformational leadership style.

IMPLICATIONS FOR LEADERS

The implications of leadership theory for educational and other administrators are rather clear. The successful leader needs to have a sound grasp of leadership theory and the skills to implement it. The principles of situational and transformational leadership theory are guides to effective administrative behavior. The leadership behavior applied to an inexperienced faculty member may be significantly different than that applied to a more experienced and tested one. Task behavior may be appropriate in dealing with a new teacher, while relationship behavior may be more appropriate when dealing with a seasoned teacher.

The four frames of leadership discussed by Bolman and Deal may be particularly helpful to school leaders and leaders in general. Consideration of the structural, human relations, political, and symbolic implications of leadership behavior can keep an administrator attuned to the various dimensions affecting appropriate leadership behavior.

With the need to deal with collective-bargaining entities, school boards, and a variety of other power issues, the political frame considerations may be particularly helpful in understanding the complexity of relationships that exist between administrators and these groups. Asking oneself the questions posed earlier under the political frame can be an effective guide to the appropriate leadership behavior in dealing with these groups.

KEY IDEAS

Recently, a plethora of research studies have been conducted on leadership and leadership styles. The overwhelming evidence indicates that there is no one singular leadership style that is most appropriate in all situations. Rather, an administrator's leadership style should be adapted to the situation so that at various times task behavior or relationship behavior might be appropriate. At other times and in other situations, various degrees of both task and relationship behavior may be most effective.

The emergence of transformational leadership has seen leadership theory come full circle. Transformational leadership theory combines aspects of the early trait theory perspective with the more current situational or contingency models. The personal charisma of the leader, along with his or her ability to formulate an organizational vision and to communicate it to others, determines the transformational leader's effectiveness.

Since the effective leader is expected to adapt his or her leadership style to an ever-changing environment, administration becomes an even more complex and challenging task. However, a thorough knowledge of leadership theory can make some sense of the apparent chaos that the administrator faces on almost a daily basis.

Among scholars, there is an assertion that *theory informs practice and practice informs theory.* This notion posits that to be an effective leader, one must base his or her practice on some form of leadership theory. If the leader consciously based his or her practice on leadership theory, this would be an example of theory informing practice. On the other hand, when a leader utilizes theory-inspired behavior that is continually ineffective, perhaps the theory must be modified to account for this deficiency. In this case, practice would be informing or modifying theory.

In this book, we will examine the leadership behavior of ten great spiritual and religious leaders, all of whom have left their mark on our global society. We will ascertain whether their behavior conforms to the principles of the Bolman/Deal situational leadership theory, and if not, whether or not the theory needs to be modified to reflect effective practice. We will also examine how these leaders' leadership practices can be applied to our own leadership behavior to make it more effective. However, before we do so, we will explore the *art* of leadership, or what I call leading with *heart*.

Chapter Two

Leading with Heart

Do unto others as you would have them do unto you.
—The Golden Rule

How the leader utilizes the concepts contained in the preceding chapter depends largely on one's philosophy of life regarding how human beings behave in the workplace. The two extremes of the continuum might be described as those leaders who believe that human beings are basically lazy and will do the very least that they need to do to "get by" in the workplace, or those who believe that people are basically industrious and, if given the choice, would opt for doing a quality job. I believe that today's most effective leaders hold the latter view.

I agree with Max De Pree, owner and CEO of the highly successful Herman Miller Furniture Company. Writing in his book *Leadership is an Art*, he says that a leader's function is to "liberate people to do what is required of them in the most effective and humane way possible." Instead of catching people doing something wrong, our goal as enlightened leaders is to catch them doing something right. I would suggest, therefore, that in addition to a rational approach to leadership, that is, leading with mind, a truly enlightened leader also leads with heart (De Pree 1989, 1).

Too often, leaders underestimate the skills and qualities of their followers. I remember Bill Faries, the chief custodian at a high school at which I was assistant principal in the mid-1970s. Bill's mother, with whom he had been extraordinarily close, had passed away after a long illness. The school was faith based and the school community went "all out" in its remembrance of Bill's mother. We held a religious service in which almost four thousand members of the school community participated. Bill, of course, was very grateful. As a token of his gratitude, he gave the school a six-by-eight-foot knitted quilt that he had personally sewn. From that point on, I did not know if Bill was a custodian who was a quilt weaver, or a quilt weaver who was a custodian.

The point is that it took the death of his mother for me and others to realize how truly talented our custodian was. So our effectiveness as leaders begins with an understanding of the diversity of people's gifts, talents, and skills. When we think about the variety of gifts that people bring to organizations and institutions, we see that leading with heart lies in cultivating, liberating, and enabling those gifts.

LEADERSHIP DEFINED

The first responsibility of a leader is to define reality through a vision. The last is to say "thank you." In between, the leader should behave like the "servant of the servants." Being a leader means having the opportunity to make a meaningful difference in the lives of those who allow leaders to lead. This summarizes what I call leading with heart. In a nutshell, these leaders don't inflict pain; they bear pain.

Whether one is a successful leader can be determined by looking at one's followers. Are they reaching their potential? Are they learning? Are they able to change without bitterness? Are they able to achieve the institution's goals and objectives? Can they manage conflict among themselves? Where the answers to these questions are an emphatic "yes," that is a place where a truly effective leader resides.

I prefer to think about leadership in terms of what the gospel writer Luke calls the "one who serves." The leader owes something to the institution he or she leads. The leader is seen in this context as steward rather than owner or proprietor. Leading with heart requires the leader to think about his or her stewardship in terms of legacy, direction, effectiveness, and values. We will come to see that virtually all of the leaders profiled in this book reflect these ideals.

LEGACY

Too many of today's leaders are interested only in immediate results that bolster their career goals. Long-range goals are left to their successors. I believe that this approach fosters autocratic leadership, which oftentimes produces short-term results but militates against creativity and its long-term benefits. In effect, this approach is the antithesis of leading with heart.

Rather, leaders should build a long-lasting legacy of accomplishment that is institutionalized for posterity. They owe their institutions and their followers a healthy existence and the relationships and reputation that enable continuity of that healthy existence. Leaders are also responsible for future leadership. They need to identify, develop, and nurture future leaders to carry on the legacy.

VALUES

Along with being responsible for providing future leaders, leaders owe the individuals in their institutions certain other legacies. Leaders need to be concerned with the institutional value system that determines the principles and standards that guide the practices of those in the organization. Leaders need to model their value systems so that the individuals in the organization can learn to transmit these values to their colleagues and to future employees. In a civilized institution, we see good manners, respect for people, and an appreciation of the way in which we serve one another. A humane, sensitive, and thoughtful leader will transmit his or her value system through his or her daily behavior. This, I believe, is what Peter Senge refers to as a "learning organization" (Senge 1990).

DIRECTION

Leaders are obliged to provide and maintain direction by developing a vision. We made the point earlier that effective leaders must leave their organizations with a legacy. Part of this legacy should be a sense of progress or momentum. An educational administrator, for instance, should imbue his or her institution with a sense of continuous progress; a sense of constant improvement. Improvement and momentum come from a clear vision of what the institution ought to be, a well-planned strategy to achieve that vision, and carefully developed and articulated directions and plans that allow everyone to participate and feel personally accountable for achieving those plans.

EFFECTIVENESS

Leaders are also responsible for institutional effectiveness by being enablers. They need to enable others to reach their potential both personally and institutionally. I believe that the most effective way of enabling one's colleagues is through participative decision making. It begins with believing in the potential of people; believing in their diversity of gifts. Leaders must realize that to maximize their own power and effectiveness, they need to empower others. Leaders are responsible for setting and attaining the goals in their organizations. Empowering or enabling others to help achieve those goals enhances the leader's chances of attaining the goals, ultimately enhancing the leader's effectiveness. Paradoxically, giving up power really amounts to gaining power.

EMPLOYEE OWNERS

We often hear managers suggest that a new program does not have a chance of succeeding unless the employees take "ownership" of the program. Most of us agree to the common sense of such an assertion. But how does a leader promote employee ownership? Let us suggest four steps as a beginning.

1. Respect people. As we have indicated earlier, this starts with appreciating the diverse gifts that individuals bring to your institution. The key is to dwell on the strengths of your coworkers, rather than on their weaknesses. Try to turn their weaknesses into strengths. This does not mean that disciplinary action or even dismissal will never become necessary. What it does mean, however, is that we should focus on the formative aspect of the employee evaluation process before we engage in the summative part.

2. Let belief guide policy and practice. We spoke earlier of developing a culture of civility in your institution. If there is an environment of mutual respect and trust, we believe that the organization will flourish. Leaders need to let their belief or value system guide their behavior. Style is merely a consequence of what we believe and what is in our hearts.

3. Recognize the need for covenants. Contractual agreements cover such things as salary, fringe benefits, and working conditions. They are part of organizational life and there is a legitimate need for them. But in today's organizations, especially educational institutions, where the best people working for these institutions are like volunteers, we need covenantal relationships. Our best workers may choose their employers. They usually choose the institution where they work based on reasons less tangible than salaries and fringe benefits. They do not need contracts, they need covenants. Covenantal relationships enable educational institutions to be civil, hospitable, and understanding of individuals' differences and unique charisms. They allow administrators to recognize that treating everyone equally is not necessarily treating everyone equitably or fairly.

4. Understand that culture counts more than structure. An educational institution that I have been associated with recently went through a particularly traumatic time when the credibility of the administration was questioned by the faculty and staff. Various organizational consultants were interviewed to facilitate a "healing" process. Most of the prospective consultants spoke of making the necessary structural changes to create a culture of trust. We finally hired a consultant whose attitude was that organizational structure has nothing to do with trust. Interpersonal relations based on mutual respect and an atmosphere of goodwill are what creates a culture of trust. Would you rather work as part of a school with an outstanding reputation or work as part of a group of outstanding individuals? Many times these two characteristics of an organization go together, but if one had to make a choice, I believe that most people would opt to work with outstanding individuals.

IT STARTS WITH TRUST, RESPECT, AND KINDNESS (HEART)

These are exciting times in education. Revolutionary steps are being taken to restructure schools and rethink the teaching–learning process. The concepts of empowerment, total quality management, the use of technology, and strategic planning are becoming the norm. However, while these activities have the potential to influence education in significantly positive ways, they must be based upon a strong foundation to achieve their full potential.

Achieving educational effectiveness is an incremental, sequential improvement process. This improvement process begins by building a sense of security within each individual so that he or she can be flexible in adapting to changes within education. Addressing only skills or techniques, such as communication, motivation, negotiation, or empowerment, is ineffective when individuals in an organization do not trust its systems, themselves, or each other. An institution's resources are wasted when invested only in training programs that assist administrators in mastering quick-fix techniques that at best attempt to manipulate, and at worst reinforce, mistrust.

The challenge is to transform relationships based on insecurity, adversarialism, and politics to those based on mutual trust. Trust is the beginning of effectiveness and forms the foundation of a principle-centered learning environment that places emphasis upon strengths and devises innovative methods to minimize weaknesses. The transformation process requires an internal locus of control that emphasizes individual responsibility and accountability for change and for promoting effectiveness.

TEAMWORK

For many of us, there exists a dichotomy between how we see ourselves as persons and how we see ourselves as workers. Ideally, that should not be. Perhaps the following words of a Zen Buddhist will be insightful:

> The master in the art of living makes little distinction
> between his work and his play, his labor and his leisure,
> his mind and his body, his education and his recreation,
> his love and his religion. He hardly knows which is which.

He simply pursues his vision of excellence in whatever he does, leaving others to decide whether he is working or playing. To him he is always doing both.

Work can be and should be productive, rewarding, enriching, fulfilling, and joyful. It is often what gets us out of bed every day. Work is one of our greatest privileges, and it is up to leaders to make certain that work is everything that it can and should be.

One way to think of work is to think of how a philosopher would lead an organization, rather than how a businessman or -woman would lead an organization. Plato's *Republic* speaks of the "philosopher-king," where the king would rule with the philosopher's ideals and values. Confucius, one of those we will profile later, also champions this approach.

Paramount among the ideals that leaders need to recognize in leading an organization is the notion of teamwork and the valuing of each individual's contribution to the final product. The synergy produced by an effective team is greater than the sum of its parts.

The foundation of the team is the recognition that each member needs every other member and no individual can be successful without the cooperation of others. As a young boy, I was a very enthusiastic baseball fan. My favorite player was the recently deceased Hall of Fame pitcher Robin Roberts of the Philadelphia Phillies. During the early 1950s, his fastball dominated the National League. My uncle, who took me to my first ballgame, explained that opposing batters were so intimidated by Roberts's fastball that they were automatic "outs" even before they got to the plate. My uncle claimed that Robin Roberts was unstoppable. Even as a young boy, I intuitively knew that no one was unstoppable by himself. I said to my uncle that I knew how to stop Robin Roberts. "Make me his catcher!"

EMPLOYEES AS VOLUNTEERS

Our institutions will not amount to anything without the people who make them what they are. And the individuals most influential in making institutions what they are, are essentially volunteers. Our very best employees can work anywhere they please. So, in a sense, they volunteer to work where they do. As leaders, we would do far better if we looked upon and treated our employees with the deference that we show our volunteers. We made the point earlier that we should treat our employees as if we had a covenantal relationship rather than a contractual relationship with them.

Aleksandr Solzhenitsyn, speaking to the 1978 graduating class of Harvard College, said this about legalistic relationships: "a society based on the letter of the law and never reaching any higher, fails to take advantage of the full range of human possibilities. The letter of the law is too cold and formal to have a beneficial influence on society. Whenever the tissue of life is woven of legalistic relationships, this creates an atmosphere of spiritual mediocrity that paralyzes men's noblest impulses." And later: "After a certain level of the problem has been reached, legalistic thinking induces paralysis; it prevents one from seeing the scale and the meaning of events" (Solzhenitsyn 1978, 17–19).

Covenantal relationships, on the other hand, induce freedom, not paralysis. As the noted psychiatrist William Glasser explains, "coercion only produces mediocrity; love or a sense of belonging produces excellence" (Glasser 1984, 167). Our goal as leaders is to encourage a covenantal relationship of love, warmth, and personal chemistry among our employee volunteers. Shared ideals, shared goals, shared respect, a sense of integrity, a sense of quality, a sense of advocacy, a sense of caring; these are the basis of an organization's covenant with its employees.

THE VALUE OF HEROES

Leading with heart requires that an organization has its share of heroes, both present and past. We have often heard individuals in various organizations say that so and so is an "institution" around here. Heroes such as these do more to influence the organizational culture of an institution than any manual or policies and procedures handbook ever could.

The senior faculty member who is recognized and respected for his or her knowledge as well as his or her humane treatment of students is a valuable asset to an educational institution. He or she is a symbol of what the institution stands for. It is the presence of these heroes that sustains the reputation of the institution and allows the workforce to feel good about itself and about where it works. The deeds and accomplishments of these heroes need to be promulgated and need to become part of the folklore of the institution.

The deeds of these heroes are usually perpetuated by the "tribal storytellers" in an organization (Bolman and Deal 1991). These are the individuals who know the history of the organization and relate it through stories of its former and current heroes. Rather than seeing them as a threat, an effective leader encourages the heroes and tribal storytellers, knowing that they are serving an invaluable role in an organization.

They work at the process of institutional renewal. They allow the institution to continuously improve. They preserve and revitalize the values of the institution. They mitigate the tendency of institutions, especially educational institutions, to become bureaucratic. These concerns are concerns of everyone in the institution, but they are the special province of the tribal storyteller. Every institution has heroes and storytellers. It is the leader's job to see to it that things like manuals and handbooks don't replace them.

THE SIGNS OF HEARTLESSNESS

Up to now we have dwelled on the characteristics of a healthy organization. In contrast, here are some of the signs that an organization is suffering from a lack of heart:

- when there is a tendency to merely "go through the motions"
- when a dark tension exists among key individuals
- when a cynical attitude prevails among employees
- when finding time to celebrate accomplishments becomes impossible
- when stories and storytellers cease
- when there is the view that one person's gain needs to be at another's expense
- when mutual trust and respect erode
- when leaders accumulate or hoard power rather than sharing it
- when attainment of short-term gains becomes detrimental to the acquisition of long-term goals
- when individuals abide by the letter of the law, but not its spirit
- when people treat students or customers as impositions
- when the accidents become more important than the substance
- when a loss of grace, style, and civility occurs
- when leaders use coercion to motivate employees
- when administrators dwell on individuals' weaknesses rather than their strengths
- when individual turf is protected to the detriment of institutional goals
- when diversity and individual gifts and charisms are not respected
- when communication is only one-way
- when employees feel exploited and manipulated
- when arrogance spawns top-down decision making
- when leaders prefer to be served rather than to serve

LEADERSHIP AS A MORAL SCIENCE

Here we address how educational administrators and other leaders should be educated and trained for their positions. Traditionally, there has been only one answer: practicing and future administrators should study educational administration in order to learn the scientific basis for decision making and to understand the scientific research that underlies proper administration.

Universities train future administrators with texts that stress the scientific research done on administrative behavior, review various studies of teacher and student performance, and provide a few techniques for accomplishing educational goals. Such approaches instill a reverence for the scientific method, but an unfortunate disregard for any humanistic and critical development of the art of administration (Foster 1986). These approaches teach us how to lead with our minds, but not necessarily with our hearts.

We are suggesting a different approach. Although there is certainly an important place for scientific research and empirically supported administrative behavior, we suggest that educational administrators also be *critical humanists* and lead with both their minds and their hearts. Humanists appreciate the usual and unusual events of our lives and engage in an effort to develop, challenge, and liberate human souls. They are critical because they are educators and are therefore not satisfied with the status quo; rather, they hope to change individuals and institutions for the better and to improve social conditions for all. We will make the argument here that an *administrative* science should be reconstructed as a *moral* science (Palestini 2011a).

An administrative science can be empirical, but it also must incorporate hermeneutic (the science of interpreting and understanding others) and critical dimensions. Social science has increasingly recognized that it must be informed by moral questions. The paradigm of natural science does not always apply when dealing with human issues. As a moral science, the science of administration would be concerned with the resolution of moral dilemmas. A critical and a literary model of administration helps to provide us with the necessary context and understanding wherein such dilemmas can be wisely resolved, and we can truly actualize our potential as administrators and leaders.

THE CRITICAL TRADITION

The so-called postpositivist leader combines the *humanist* tradition with *critical* theory. Dissatisfaction with current empirical administrative approaches for examining social life stems from these approaches' inability to deal with questions of value and morality.

For example, Daniel Griffiths and Peter Ribbins (1995) criticize orthodox theories because they "ignore the presence of unions and fail to account for the scarcity of women and minorities in top administrative positions" (3). David Ericson and Frederick Ellett (2002) ask, "Why had educational research had so few real implications for educational policy?" One answer is that an empiricist research program modeled on the natural sciences fails to address issues of understanding and interpretation. This failure precludes researchers from reaching a genuine understanding of the human condition. It is time, these scholars argue, to treat educational research as a moral science (525–46).

The term "moral" is being used here in its cultural, professional, spiritual, and ethical sense, not necessarily a religious sense. The moral side of administration has to do with the *dilemmas* that face us in education and other professions. All educators face at least three areas of dilemmas: control, curricular, and societal. Control dilemmas involve the resolution of classroom management and control issues, particularly the issue of who is in charge and to what degree.

Similar dilemmas occur in the curricular domain and relate to whether the curriculum is considered as received, public knowledge where the child is a passive recipient, or whether it is considered private, individualized knowledge, of the type achieved through discoveries and experiments, and where the child is an active participant. These curricular difficulties also depend on whether one conceives of the child as customer or as an individual. The customer receives professional services generated from a body of knowledge, whereas the individual receives personal services generated from his or her particular needs and context.

A final set of dilemmas has to do with what children bring to school and how they are to be treated once there. One concerns the distribution of teacher resources. Should one focus more resources on the less talented, in order to bring them up to standards, or on the more talented, in order for them to reach their full potential? The same question arises in regard to the distribution of justice. Should classroom rules be applied uniformly without regard to the differing circumstances of each child, or should family background, economic factors, and other sociological influences be considered? Should a teacher stress a common culture or ethnic differences and subculture consciousness?

Much of teaching and leading involves resolving these dilemmas by making a variety of decisions throughout the school day. Such decisions can be made in a *reflective* or an *unreflective* way. An unreflective manner means simply teaching as one was taught, without giving consideration to available alternatives. A reflective approach involves an examination of the widest array of alternatives.

This same logic can be applied to administration. Administration involves the resolution of various dilemmas, that is, the making of moral decisions. As with teaching, one set of dilemmas involves control. How much participation can teachers have in the administration of the school? How much participation can parents and students have? Who evaluates and for what purpose? Is the role of administration collegial or authority centered? The area of the curriculum brings up similar questions. Is the school oriented to basic skills, advanced skills, social skills, or all three? Should the curricula be teacher made or national, state, or system mandated? Should student evaluation be based on teacher assessment or standardized tests? What is authentic assessment?

Other dilemmas pertain to the idea of schooling in society. Should the schools be oriented to ameliorate cognitive and environmental deficits that some students bring with them, or should they "stick to the three Rs?" Should schools be seen as agents of change, oriented to the creation of a more just society, or as socializers that adapt the young to the current social structure?

Oftentimes, these questions are answered unreflectively and simply resolved on an "as needed" basis. This approach often resolves the dilemma but does not foster a real *transformation* in one's self, role, or institution. If administration and leadership encompasses transformation, and I would argue that it should, then an additional lens to structural functionalism must be found through which these questions can be viewed. I suggest that the additional lens be in the form of critical humanism and/or the Ignatian Vision or some other moral lens—the point being that if leaders expect to reach their potential, some type of moral guide needs to be consciously in place.

THE IGNATIAN HERMENEUTIC (LENS)

In addition to the critical humanist lens, another moral lens through which we can view our leadership behavior to ensure that we are leading with heart is the Ignatian Vision. More than 450 years ago, Ignatius of Loyola, a young priest born to a Spanish aristocratic family, founded the Society of Jesus, the Jesuits, and wrote his seminal book *The Spiritual Exercises* (Loyola 2007).

In this book, he suggested a "way of life" and a "way of looking at things" that has been propagated by his religious community and his other followers for almost five centuries. His principles have been utilized in a variety of ways. They have been used as an aid in developing one's own spiritual life; to formulate a way of learning that has become the curriculum and instructional method employed in the sixty high schools and the twenty-eight Jesuit colleges and universities in the United States; and to develop individual administrative style. Together, these principles comprise the *Ignatian Vision* or hermeneutic.

There are five Ignatian principles that we will explore here as a foundation for developing a moral frame and an administrative philosophy and leadership style: (1) The Ignatian concept of the *magis*, or the "more"; (2) his concept of *cura personalis*, or "care of the person"; (3) the process of *inquiry* or *discernment*; (4) the development of *men and women for others*; and (5) service to the *underserved* and marginalized, or his concept of *social justice*.

At the core of the Ignatian Vision is the concept of the *magis*, or the "more." Ignatius spent the greater part of his life seeking perfection in all areas of his personal, spiritual, and professional life. He was never satisfied with the mediocrity of the status quo. He was constantly seeking to improve his own spiritual life, as well as his secular life as leader of a growing religious community. He was an advocate of "continuous improvement" long before it became a corporate slogan, long before Edwards Deming used it to develop his Total Quality Management approach to management, and long before Japan used it to revolutionize its economy after World War II.

The idea of constantly seeking "the more" implies change. The *magis* is a movement away from the status quo; and moving away from the status quo defines change. The Ignatian Vision requires individuals and institutions to embrace the process of change as a vehicle for personal and institutional improvement. For his followers, frontiers and boundaries are not obstacles or ends, but new challenges to be faced, new opportunities to be welcomed.

Thus, change needs to become a way of life. Ignatius further implores his followers to "be the change that you expect in others." In other words, we are called to model desired behavior—to live out our values, to be of ever fuller service to our communities, and to aspire to the more universal good. Ignatius had no patience with mediocrity. He constantly strove for the greater good.

The *magis* principle, then, can be described as the main norm in the selection of information and the interpretation of it. Every real alternative for choice must be conducive to the advancement toward perfection. When some aspect of a particular alternative is *more* conducive to reaching perfection than other alternatives, we have reason to choose that alternative. Earlier, we spoke of the "dilemmas" that educators face during every working day. The *magis* principle is a "way of seeing" that can help us in selecting the better alternative.

How one moves toward achieving the *magis* is closely related to one's ability to utilize the Ignatian principle of *discernment.* In his writings, Ignatius urges us to challenge the status quo through the methods of inquiry and discernment.

To Ignatius, the need to enter into inquiry and discernment is to determine God's will. However, this same process is of value for the purely *secular* purpose of deciding on which "horn of a dilemma" one should come down. To aid us in utilizing inquiry and discernment as useful tools in challenging the status quo and determining the right choice to be made, Ignatius suggests that the ideal disposition for engaging in inquiry and discernment is humility rather than hubris or arrogance. The disposition of humility is especially helpful when, despite one's best efforts, the evidence that one alternative is more conducive to the betterment of society is not compelling.

When the discerner cannot find evidence to show that one alternative is more conducive to the common good, Ignatius calls for a judgment in favor of what more assimilates the discerner's life to the life of service and humility. Thus, Ignatius is suggesting that when the *greatest* good cannot readily be determined, the *greater* good is more easily discerned in a position of humility.

Ignatius presents us with several other norms for facing our "dilemmas." In choices that directly affect the individual person and the underserved or marginalized, especially the poor, Ignatius urges us to give preference to those in need. This brings us to his next guiding principle, *cura personalis*, or care of the person.

Another of Ignatius' important and enduring principles is his notion that, despite the primacy of the common good, the need to care for the individual person should never be lost. From the very beginning, the *cura personalis* principle has been included in the mission statement of virtually every high school and college founded by the Jesuits. It also impacts the method of instruction suggested for all Jesuit schools in the *Ratio Studiorum*, or the "course of study." Thus, a Jesuit education is primarily student-centered rather than teacher-centered.

All Jesuit educational institutions are to foster what we now refer to as a "constructivist" classroom, where the student is an active participant in the learning process. This contrasts with the "transmission" method of instruction where the teacher is paramount, and the student is a passive participant in the process.

This *cura* principle also has implications for how we conduct ourselves as educational administrators. Ignatius calls us to value the gifts and charisms of our colleagues and to address any deficiencies that they might have and turn them into strengths. For example, during the employee-evaluation process, Ignatius would urge us to focus on the formative or developmental stage of the evaluation far more than on the summative or contract renewal/nonrenewal stage.

The fourth principle that we wish to consider is the Ignatian concept of service. Once again, this principle has been propagated from the very outset. The expressed goal of virtually every Jesuit institution is "to develop men and women with and for others." Jesuit institutions are called on to create a culture of service as one way of ensuring that the students, faculty, and staff of these institutions reflect the educational, civic, and spiritual values of the Ignatian Vision.

Institutions following the Ignatian tradition of service to others have done so primarily through community-service programs, and more recently, service learning. Service to the community provides students and others with a means of helping others, a way to put their value system into action, and a tangible way to assist local communities. Although these are valuable benefits, up until recently there was no formal integration of the service experience into the curriculum and no formal introspection concerning the impact of service on the individual.

During the last twenty years there has been a movement toward creating a more intentional academic relationship. Service has evolved from a modest student activity into an exciting pedagogical opportunity. In the past, service was viewed as a cocurricular activity; today it plays an integral role in the learning process. For example, at many of today's colleges and universities, accounting majors help senior citizens complete their income tax returns—thus applying their academic expertise to their service.

The implications of "service to others" for administration are clear. Not only can educational administrators enhance their effectiveness by including the idea of service to others in their curricula, but also by modeling it in their personal and professional lives. The concept of administrators becoming the "servant of the servants" is what Ignatius had in mind here. Servant leaders do not inflict pain, they bear pain, and they treat their employees as "volunteers," a concept explored earlier.

The Ignatian concept of "service" leads into his notion of solidarity with the underserved and marginalized and his principle of *social justice*. We begin with an attempt to achieve some measure of clarity on the nature and role of social justice in the Ignatian Vision. According to some, Ignatius defined justice in both a narrow and wide sense (Toner 1991). In the *narrow* sense, it is "justice among men and women" that is involved. In this case, it is a matter of "clear obligations" among "members of the human family." The application of this kind of justice would include not only the rendering of material goods, but also immaterial goods such as "reputation, dignity, the possibility of exercising freedom" (Tripole 1994).

Many of his followers also believe Ignatius defined justice in a *wider* sense "where situations are encountered which are humanly intolerable and demand a remedy" (Tripole 1994). Here the situations may be a product of "explicitly unjust acts" caused by "clearly identified people" who cannot be commanded to correct the injustices, yet the dignity of the human person requires that justice be restored; or they may be caused by nonidentifiable people.

It is precisely within the structural forces of inequality in society where injustice of this second type is found, where injustice is "institutionalized"; that is, built into economic, social, and political structures both national and international, and where people are suffering from poverty and hunger, from the unjust distribution of wealth, resources, and power. As we shall see, the leadership behavior of Pope Francis I, a Jesuit who is profiled in this book, is based on this wider definition of social justice.

It is almost certain that Ignatius did not only concern himself with injustices that were purely economic. He often cites injustices about "threats to human life and it quality," "racial and political discrimination," and loss of respect for the "rights of individuals or groups." When one adds to these the "vast range of injustices" enumerated in his writings, one sees that the Ignatian Vision understands its mission of justice to include "the widest possible view of justice," involving every area where there is an attack on human rights (Chapple 1993).

Implications for Administration

Each of the principles of the Ignatian Vision noted above has a variety of implications for leaders. The *magis* principle has implications for administrators in that it calls for us to continually seek perfection in all that we do. In effect, this means that we must seek to continually improve, always striving for the greater good. And, since improvement implies change, we need to be champions of needed change in our institutions. This means that we have to model a tolerance for change and embrace not only our own change initiatives, but also those in other parts of the organization. In effect, the Ignatian Vision prompts us not to be merely leaders but transformational leaders.

The principle of *cura personalis* has additional implications. To practice the Ignatian Vision, one must treat people with dignity under all circumstances. *Cura personalis* also requires us to extend ourselves in offering individual attention and attending to the needs of all those in whom we come in contact. Being sensitive to the individual's unique needs is particularly required. Many times in our efforts to treat people equally, we fail to treat them fairly or equitably. Certain individuals have greater needs than others, and many times satisfying these needs requires exceptions to be made on their behalf.

For example, if a colleague does not complete an assignment on time, but the tardiness is due to the fact that he or she is going through some personal or family trauma at the moment, the principle of *cura personalis* calls on us to make an exception in this case. It is likely that some would consider such an exception to be unfair to those who made the effort to complete their assignments in a timely manner, or that we cannot possibly be sensitive to the special needs of all of our colleagues. However, as long as the exception is made for everyone in the same circumstances, Ignatius would not perceive this exception as being unfair. In fact, the exception would be expected if one is practicing the principle of "care of the person."

The Ignatian process of *discernment* requires educational administrators to be reflective practitioners. It calls on us to be introspective regarding our administrative and leadership behavior. We are asked to reflect on the ramifications of our decisions, especially in light of their cumulative effect on the equitable distribution of power and on the marginalized individuals and groups in our communities. In effect, the principle of discernment galvanizes the other principles embodied in the Ignatian Vision. During the discernment process, we are asked to reflect upon how our planned behavior will manifest the *magis* principle, *cura personalis*, and service to the community, especially the underserved, marginalized, and oppressed.

The development of men and women for others requires one to have his or her own sense of service toward those with whom the leader interacts, and that one also develop this spirit of service in others. The concept of "servant leadership" requires us to encourage others toward a life and career of service and to assume the position of being the "servant of the servants." As noted earlier, Ignatius thinks about leadership in terms of what the gospel writer Luke calls the "one who serves." The leader owes something to the institution he or she leads. The leader is seen in this context as steward rather than owner or proprietor.

The implications of Ignatius' notion of social justice are myriad for a leader. Being concerned about the marginalized among our constituencies is required. We are called to be sensitive to those individuals and groups that do not share equitably in the distribution of power and influence. In a school setting, these persons might be the secretaries and the custodians, or even the students' parents. Distinctions according to race, class, gender, and status should never be tolerated. Participative decision making and collaborative behavior are encouraged among administrators imbued with the Ignatian Vision.

Equitable representation of all segments of the school community should be provided whenever feasible. Leadership enactments such as these will assure that the dominant culture is not perpetuated to the detriment of the minority culture, rendering the minorities powerless. We will find in the succeeding chapters that the heroic leaders profiled there consciously or unconsciously incorporate many of the Ignatian concepts into their leadership behavior.

Thus, in my view, the Ignatian Vision in the form of a moral frame *completes* situational leadership theory. Left on its own, situational leadership theory is secular and amoral. Utilizing situational leadership theory alone is as likely to produce a leader in the mold of Adolf Hitler, Joseph Stalin, or Slobodan Milosevic as it is to produce a leader in the mold of the ten leaders profiled here. But the use of the additional lens of the Ignatian Vision or some other moral frame through which to view our situational leadership behavior will ensure that we have more leaders who use their talents in the pursuit of good and fewer who use their talents for evil purposes.

KEY IDEAS

I began this book by suggesting that leaders are made, not born. I posited that if one could master the *technical* skills involved in effective leadership, one could become a successful administrator. In this chapter, however, we make the assertion that learning the skills involved in effective leadership is only part of the story. Leadership is as much an art, a belief, a condition of the heart, as it is mastering a set of skills and understanding leadership theory. A truly successful and heroic leader, therefore, is one who leads with both the *mind* and the *heart.*

When we look at the leadership behavior of the leaders included in this study, we should observe not only if their leadership practices conform to the Bolman and Deal situational leadership model, but also if they are leading with *heart.* I believe that we will find that those leaders who are most comfortable consistently operating out of Bolman and Deal's human resource and symbolic frames and my moral frame of leadership are most likely to be leading with heart. The most effective leaders will then be those who lead with both mind (structural, political frames) and heart (human resource, symbolic frames) and view their leadership behavior through the lens of the Ignatian Vision or some similar moral frame.

Chapter Three

Moses

Let my people go!

—Moses

BACKGROUND

Born about 1390 BC, Moses is a prophet in the religious tradition of Abraham. According to the Hebrew Bible, he was a former Egyptian citizen who later became the religious and political leader of the Jewish nation. He is considered to be the most important prophet in Judaism, having been recognized as the author of the first five books of the Bible known as the Torah.

According to the Book of Exodus, Moses lived during the time when his people, the Israelites, were enslaved under the rule of the Egyptian Pharaoh. Out of fear that the increasing population of Israelites in the region might foment revolt, the Pharaoh, Ramses, ordered that all newborn Hebrew boys be killed. In order to save him from death, Moses's mother hid her newborn in a cradle and placed him in the bulrushes along the Nile River. The child was found by the Pharaoh's daughter and raised in the palace of the royal family.

After killing an Egyptian slavemaster who was physically abusing the Jewish slaves, Moses fled across the Red Sea to Midian to avoid prosecution. While in Midian, Moses encountered the God of Israel speaking to him in the form of a burning bush. According to Jewish tradition, God then ordered Moses to return to Egypt to demand the release of the Israelites from slavery.

The Pharaoh initially refused, but after experiencing the historically famous Ten Plagues (rivers turned to blood, frogs covered Egypt, hail storms, fire, boils, perpetual darkness, gadflies and other pestilence, the death of the Egyptian livestock, the storm of locusts, and the angel of death killing the

Egyptian firstborns), Ramses let the Israelites leave Egypt. After Ramses had second thoughts, however, his army pursued the fleeing Israelites, which precipitated the legendary story of the parting of the Red Sea. In order for the Israelites to escape from Egypt, they had to cross the Red Sea. While in close pursuit, the Egyptian army was engulfed in the closing rapids after Moses asked God to part the Red Sea so that the Israelites could escape.

After the Exodus from Egypt and the crossing of the Red Sea, Moses led the Israelites to Mount Sinai where he received the Ten Commandments. But when Moses returned from the mountain, he found the Israelites worshiping the golden calf. Angered by this worshiping of false gods, Moses concluded that the Israelites were not yet ready to enter the Promised Land.

While at Sinai, however, the Israelites entered into a covenant agreeing to obey God's laws. After forty years of wandering in the desert, Moses passed away within sight of the much anticipated Promised Land. It remained up to his brother, Aaron, and his general, Joshua, to lead the Israelites to the Promised Land (Malherbe and Ferguson 1978).

SITUATIONAL LEADERSHIP ANALYSIS

Situational models of leadership differ from earlier trait and behavioral models in asserting that no single way of leading works in all situations. Rather, appropriate behavior depends on the circumstances at a given time. Effective managers diagnose the situation, identify the leadership style or behavior that will be most effective, and then determine whether they can implement the required style.

As we shall see, there were a number of instances where Moses showed himself to be a situational leader. He demonstrated his structural frame leanings when he enforced the Ten Commandments with the Israelites and made them remain in the desert for forty years because they worshiped the golden calf. On the other hand, he showed his human resource frame tendencies when he distributed the manna in the dessert according to need rather than equally.

Moses engaged in symbolic frame leadership behavior when he wrote the Torah, using their past history as an inspiration to the Israelites. And Moses used his political frame talents in managing the many internal disputes that the Hebrews had with one another over their years in the desert. Finally, there is no question that Moses engaged in the moral frame in that the Ten Commandments, which he accepted from the God of Israel, remain to this day the code of conduct for billions of people around the globe.

THE STRUCTURAL FRAME

Structural frame leaders seek to develop a new model of the relationship of structure, strategy, and environment for their organizations. Strategic planning, extensive preparation, and effecting change are priorities for them.

Moses was very active in the structural frame. Early on, he used structural frame behavior in the extreme in killing an Egyptian slavemaster who was physically abusing a Hebrew slave. Later, he utilized the structural frame when at his command the Ten Plagues descended upon Egypt and in leading the Israelites out of Egyptian bondage to Mount Sinai, where he received and enforced adherence to the Ten Commandments. And in a state of anger over the Jews worshiping the golden calf, he engaged in structural frame behavior once again in demanding that the Jews remain in the desert for forty years as penance for their idolatry before bringing them to the brink of entering the Promised Land.

Moses utilized the structural frame when he met with the Hebrew elders and entered into a covenant by which the Israelites would become the children of God and obey his laws. He also used structural frame leadership behavior in a more dramatic way when he led the Israelites in a battle against the neighboring Amalekites. In that battle, Moses used a new strategy that is still used today. While Joshua, who was to succeed Moses and Aaron in leading the Israelites to the Promised Land, led the army, Moses would stand on the hilltop away from the front lines and direct the battle from there (Malherbe and Ferguson 1978).

THE HUMAN RESOURCE FRAME

Human resource leaders believe in people and communicate that belief. They are passionate about productivity through people. Moses engaged in the archetypical display of human resource frame behavior by leading the Israelites out of slavery in Egypt and into the Promised Land of milk and honey. But there are other instances when Moses utilized human resource frame leadership enactments.

For example, when the Israelites were starving in the desert and God sent them sustenance in the form of manna from heaven, Moses directed that the manna not be distributed equally but according to need "so that the stronger did not have a surplus nor was the weaker deprived of his fair share" (Malherbe and Ferguson 1978, 40). And in one final display of human resource frame behavior, rather than leading the Israelites into the Promised Land himself before he died, Moses humbly allowed his brother, Aaron, and his general, Joshua, to do so.

THE SYMBOLIC FRAME

In the symbolic frame, the organization is seen as a stage, a theater in which every actor plays certain roles, and the symbolic leader attempts to communicate the right impressions to the right audiences. This is a frame in which Moses excelled. Such universally recognized symbolic frame enactments as the burning bush, the ten plagues, the passover, the parting of the Red Sea, the Exodus from Egypt, the Ten Commandments, the worshiping of the golden calf, manna from heaven, the covenant, the promised land, and the Torah are all attributed to Moses. Suffice it to say, Moses left us with a considerable legacy of symbolic frame leadership behavior.

THE POLITICAL FRAME

Leaders operating out of the political frame clarify what they want and what they can get. Political leaders are realists above all. They never let what they want cloud their judgment about what is possible. They assess the distribution of power and interests. They are most interested in "making friends and influencing people."

Although not one of his prolific frames, there is evidence that Moses did operate out of the political frame when the situation called for it. While the Israelites lived in the desert for forty years, Moses had many opportunities to display political frame leadership behavior. In one instance when two Hebrews fought with one another, Moses tried to restrain them, counseling that because they were brothers, they should "make nature and not passion the arbiter of their disputes" (Malherbe and Ferguson 1978, 34).

On another occasion, when it was concluded that the Israelites by themselves were not capable of conducting their own affairs, "a petition was brought before Moses that the law be mediated through him, on the grounds that the people had no doubt that he would be inspired by God to do the right thing" (Malherbe and Ferguson 1978, 43).

THE MORAL FRAME

As mentioned earlier, the moral frame is my own contribution to situational leadership theory. In my view, the moral frame completes situational leadership theory. Without it, leaders could just as easily use their leadership skills for promoting evil as for promoting good. Leaders operating out of the moral frame are concerned about their obligations and responsibilities to their followers. Moral frame leaders use some type of moral compass to direct their behavior. They practice what has been described as servant leadership and are concerned with those individuals and groups that are marginalized in their organizations and in society. In short, they are concerned about social justice.

Just the mention of the Ten Commandments should be evidence enough that like virtually every religious/spiritual leader profiled in this study, Moses possessed a keen moral lens through which he filtered his leadership behavior. It is obvious that he used his considerable leadership acumen in the pursuit of the greater good.

KEY IDEAS

As we have seen, Moses personifies a leader operating out of the situational leadership mode. He readily adapted his leadership behavior to the situation before him. He utilized all five frames suggested. His dominant tendency may have been the symbolic frame, but when the situation called for it, he seemed perfectly willing to utilize the other four frames. Although one could criticize his radical use of the structural frame in the form of killing in self-defense, his overall use of situational leadership theory was effective and exemplary.

Chapter Four

Gautama Buddha

Writing is good, thinking is better. Cleverness is good, patience is better.
—*Gautama Buddha*

BACKGROUND

Gautama Buddha, also known as Siddhartha Gautama, was a sage upon whose teachings the Buddhist religion was founded. He was born about 500 BC in Lumbini (present-day Nepal) and taught the lesson of the Golden Mean or the Middle Way between complete indulgence and severe asceticism. He was of royal heritage and was expected to follow in the footsteps of his parents and become a ruler of a local tribe.

When Gautama was sixteen, he was married to a cousin of the same age, and the couple had at least one child. Even though he was of royal blood and lived an upper-class childhood, the future Buddha felt early on that material wealth and great power should not be man's ultimate goals.

At age twenty-nine, Gautama left the palace and began a pilgrimage to discern the real meaning of life. He renounced the life of a royal and became an ascetic and went on to study yoga. After mastering the art of yogic meditation, he was twice offered positions to succeed his teachers but demurred both times, preferring to continue his search for "enlightenment" or an "awakening." But upon discovering that extreme asceticism was not the way, he came upon what Buddhists refer to as the "Middle Way."

According to Buddhist belief, after a reputed forty-nine days of meditation, Gautama experienced an "awakening" whereby he discovered the cause of suffering and pain and the steps necessary to eliminate it. These discoveries are known as the "Four Noble Truths" and are at the foundation of Buddhist belief. The mastery of the four truths brings one to the supreme state of liberation or freedom known as "Nirvana." According to Gautama, if one can free himself from ignorance, greed, hatred, and other afflictions, Nirvana or a perfect peace of mind would be realized.

For the remaining forty-five years of his life, Gautama Buddha traveled all over southern India teaching his belief and attracting thousands of disciples. The Buddha passed away at about the age of eighty, and on his deathbed he is famously believed to have instructed his disciples to follow one of his most stringent credos, namely to "follow no leader" (Hesse 1951).

SITUATIONAL LEADERSHIP ANALYSIS

Situational models of leadership differ from earlier trait and behavioral models in asserting that no single way of leading works in all situations. Rather, appropriate behavior depends on the circumstances at a given time. Effective managers diagnose the situation, identify the leadership style or behavior that will be most effective, and then determine whether they can implement the required style.

There are several instances when Gautama Buddha showed his inclination toward situational leadership theory. He possessed a flexible attitude and was often willing to adapt to differing circumstances. One of his famous quotes showed his flexibility: "Let us enjoy this fruit and await further ones, Govinda [his companion]. This fruit for which we are already indebted to Gotama [a prophet], consists in the fact that he has enticed us away from the Samanas [a religious sect]. Whether there are still other and better fruits, let us patiently wait and see" (Hesse 1951, 19).

In his quest for perfection, Gautama was always willing to change course when the situation called for it. For a long time, like the Amish and Mennonites, Gautama lived *in* the world without really being *of* the world. His senses, which he had deadened during the early years, were awakened. Despite retaining some of the principles of his early lifestyle (a moderate life, pleasure in thinking, hours of meditation, knowledge of the self, of the eternal self that was neither body nor consciousness), he now learned to transact business affairs, to exercise power over people, to have romantic relations with women, to wear fine clothes, and to take scented baths. In time, however, this lifestyle became old. But in true situational frame form, he once again returned to a life of asceticism.

The process of this rebirth or reincarnation took on a situational face. After enduring a bout of hopelessness over his misdirected life, Gautama contemplated suicide. Then, from a remote part of his soul, he heard a sound. It was one word, one syllable. The ancient beginning and ending of all Brahmin prayers, the holy Om, which had the meaning of "the Perfect One" or "Perfection." At that moment, when the sound of Om reached his ears, his suffering soul suddenly awakened and he recognized the error of his ways and resolved to reform his life (Hesse 1951, 72).

Another indication of Gautama's willingness to adapt his leadership enactments to the situation involved his son. It turns out that his son had, in effect, become a prodigal son and lived a life of depravity. Gautama learned the situational nature of being a parent and concluded that he had been too indulgent with his son and changed his tactics, maybe too drastically. After enduring Gautama's rather extreme structural frame leadership behavior, his son ran away from home, never to return.

But the experience with his son changed Gautama once again. He now regarded people in a different light. He began to combine structural frame behavior with human resource frame behavior, and he became humbler and more curious, sympathetic, and warm in his relations with others. No longer did their vanities, desires, and trivialities bother him. In fact, he came to appreciate that this ambivalence to others' differences accelerated one's way to reaching the perfect state of "Nirvana."

THE STRUCTURAL FRAME

Structural frame leaders seek to develop a new model of the relationship of structure, strategy, and environment for their organizations. Strategic planning, extensive preparation, and effecting change are priorities for them.

Gautama demonstrated his tendency to utilize the structural frame at an early age. Even as a youngster, he displayed his intelligence and thirst for knowledge. He had already taken part in the learned men's discussions and had engaged in debate with his lifelong companion, Govinda, and had practiced the art of contemplation and meditation and learned how to pronounce what would become a sacred word in the Buddhist faith, the "Om."

Gautama displayed his structural frame side in being very strong-willed at times. Once he made up his mind, he was determined to move forward. "We will not waste words, Govinda," he said softly. "Tomorrow at daybreak I will begin the life of the Samanas [type of Buddhist]. Let us not discuss it again" (Hesse 1951, 7).

Gautama used structural frame leadership behavior in narrowing his vision down to one single goal—"to become empty; to become empty of thirst, desire, dreams, pleasure and sorrow—to let the self die, no longer to be self, to experience the peace of the emptied heart, to experience pure thought" (Hesse 1951, 11).

Instructed by the eldest of the Samanas, Gautama practiced self-denial and meditation according to their rules. When this process did not progress to his satisfaction, Gautama once again utilized structural frame behavior and adopted a more materialistic process. "It does not appear so to me," he said to his companion, "that what I have learned so far from the Samanas, I could have learned more quickly and easily in every inn in the prostitutes' quarter, among the carriers and dice players. Flight from self is a temporary escape from the torment of self" (Hesse 1951, 13).

Upon leaving his mentor, Gotama, Gautama Buddha used structural frame language by declaring: "You have learned nothing through knowledge, through enlightenment. You have learned nothing through teaching, and so I think, O Illustrious One, that nobody finds salvation through teaching. That is why I am going on my way—not to seek another and better doctrine for I know there is none, but to leave all doctrines and all teachings to reach my goal alone—or die." Then, in order not to burn any bridges, Gautama sprinkled in a little political frame behavior and ended by saying, "But I will often remember this day, O Illustrious One, and this hour when my eyes behold a holy man" (Hesse 1951, 28).

After the death of Gotama, Gautama Buddha had a change of heart and again practiced structural frame behavior in adopting yet another philosophy of life. In responding to his erstwhile companion Govinda's question about whether he had a doctrine or belief that helped him live and do right, he said: "You know I have come to distrust doctrine and teachers and to turn my back on them. . . . I have had thought and knowledge here and there. But this one thought has impressed me. Wisdom is not communicable. The wisdom which a wise man tries to communicate always sounds foolish. Knowledge can be communicated, but not wisdom. Therefore, teachings are of no use to me; they have no hardness, no softness, nor colors, no corners, no smell, no taste—they have nothing but words. Thus, love is the most important thing in the world . . . With a great teacher, the thing to me that is of greater importance than the words; his deeds and life are more important than his talk" (Hesse 1951, 119).

THE HUMAN RESOURCE FRAME

Human resource leaders believe in people and communicate that belief. They are passionate about productivity through people. Since Gautama Buddha dedicated his life to finding a way to inner peace that he could share with everyone on the earthly pilgrimage to heaven, it is not surprising that he frequently operated out of the human resource frame.

There are a number of documented stories testifying to Gautama's use of human resource frame leadership behavior. One such instance was a time when he gave his clothes to a poor Brahmin on the road, retaining only his simple loincloth. And he routinely gave any excess food that he had to the poor. Historical accounts indicate that he was accessible and welcomed everyone who was brought to him. "The merchant who brought him linen for sale was welcome; the debtor who sought a loan was welcome; the beggar was welcome who stayed an hour telling him the story of his poverty and who was yet not as poor as Gautama was welcome," said one his disciples (Hesse 1951, 57).

When his longtime companion, Govinda, decided to leave Gautama's side and become a disciple of another holy man, Gautama again showed his human resource frame side and was happy for him. "Often I have thought: Will Govinda ever take a step without me, on his own conviction? Now, you are a man and have chosen your own path. May you go along it to the end, my friend, and may you find salvation," he said to him (Hesse 1951, 24).

THE SYMBOLIC FRAME

In the symbolic frame, the organization is seen as a stage, a theater in which every actor plays certain roles, and the symbolic leader attempts to communicate the right impressions to be the right audiences. As we shall see, Gautama Buddha was an inspirational figure and frequently operated out of the symbolic frame.

Gautama indicated the value that he placed on symbolic frame leadership behavior when he observed that being an ascetic and fasting and philosophizing were not in and of themselves very useful, but he explained that they were necessary enactments because of their symbolic value and their indication of deeper qualities. "You see, the day before yesterday," he said to one of his followers, "I was still an unkempt beggar; but yesterday I kissed my first lady and soon I will be a merchant and have money and all those things which you value. So, everyone can seek his goal, if he can think, wait and fast" (Hesse 1951, 37).

Another display of symbolic frame behavior took place during his materialistic phase, when upon being interviewed for a position as a merchant, he was handed a sheet of paper and a pen and asked to write something to demonstrate that he could read and write. Gautama wrote the following: "Writing is good, thinking is better. Cleverness is good, patience is better." Gautama was hired on the spot.

Once he decided that the life of an ascetic was not the best way of reaching Nirvana, Gautama engaged in symbolic frame leadership behavior to show his followers what should be done. Now that he realized that his inward voice had been right, that no teacher alone could have brought him to salvation, he decided that to reach a state of Nirvana, one needed to first experience the real world and lose one's self at least temporarily in a life of "power, women, and money"; that was why he had to be a merchant, a gambler, a drinker, and a man of property so that the innocence would die.

Then, according to Gautama, one would be reborn with the attitude of a child and have a better chance of reaching Nirvana (Hesse 1951, 81).

Gautama further elucidated this concept with symbolic frame behavior in the form of an allegory of a ferryman. Gautama would often reminisce with his followers about his encounter with a ferryman that would change his life. "Will you accept these rich clothes from me . . . for I have no money to pay you for taking me across the river?" Gautama asked the ferryman. The ferryman not only gave Gautama a free ride, he invited him to live with him and became Gautama Buddha's first disciple. "Something emanated from the ferry and from the ferryman that many were motivated to confess their transgressions and asked for comfort and advice," he said. Thus, the life of a generous, altruistic, and peace-loving ferryman became a Buddhist ideal (Hesse 1951, 85).

THE POLITICAL FRAME

Leaders operating out of the political frame clarify what they want and what they can get. Political leaders are realists above all. They never let what they want cloud their judgment about what is possible. They assess the distribution of power and interests. They are most interested in "making friends and influencing people." None of the leaders in this book would have reached the level of influence that they have without engaging in at least a modicum of political frame behavior in their lives, and Gautama Buddha was no exception.

When Gautama decided to abandon his relationship with his first mentor, Gotama, he did not burn any bridges. After announcing to Gotama that he was seeking an even greater mentor, he leavened the situation with a little political frame behavior and declared to his companion: "Now I will show the old man that I have learned something from him." Gautama went on to hypnotize Gotama, a skill that he had indeed learned from the holy man (Hesse 1951, 19).

When Gautama Buddha was seeking a rich patron to fund his mission, his lady friend introduced him to a wealthy merchant named Kamaswami. "He is the richest merchant in town," she said. "If you please him, he will take you into his service," she advised. "Be friendly towards him; he is becoming old and indolent. If you please him, he will place great confidence in you," which is exactly what Gautama Buddha did (Hesse 1951, 50).

In one last example of Gautama's occasional and appropriate use of political frame behavior, upon being reprimanded by Kamaswami for returning late from the village in which he was working, Gautama defended his taking time to talk to the villagers and making friends there. "If I ever go there again, perhaps to buy a later harvest, or for some other purpose, friendly people will receive me and I will be glad that I did not previously display hastiness and displeasure (Hesse 1951, 56).

THE MORAL FRAME

As mentioned earlier, the moral frame is my own contribution to situational leadership theory. In my view, the moral frame completes situational leadership theory. Without it, leaders could just as easily use their leadership skills for promoting evil as for promoting good. Leaders operating out of the moral frame are concerned about their obligations and responsibilities to their followers. Moral frame leaders use some type of moral compass to direct their behavior. They practice what has been described as servant leadership and are concerned with those individuals and groups that are marginalized in their organizations and in society. In short, they are concerned about social justice.

The lifelong quest to reach the state of Nirvana should be evidence enough that like virtually every religious/spiritual leader profiled in this study, Gautama Buddha possessed a moral lens through which he filtered his leadership behavior. It is obvious that he used his considerable leadership acumen in the lifelong pursuit of the virtues of inner peace and tranquility.

KEY IDEAS

As we have seen, Gautama Buddha personifies a leader operating out of the situational leadership mode. He readily adapted his leadership behavior to the situation before him. He utilized all five frames suggested. Like many of the leaders profiled here, his dominant tendency may have been the symbolic frame, but when the situation called for it, he seemed perfectly willing to utilize the other four frames.

In addition to the millions of Buddhists around the world, Gautama Buddha's leadership enactments greatly influenced the leadership styles of such luminaries as Mahatma Gandhi and Martin Luther King Jr. We would all do well to consider modeling some of our own leadership enactments after those of the so-called "Illustrious One," Gautama Buddha.

Chapter Five

Confucius

Do not do to others what you do not want done to yourself [Silver Rule].
—*Confucius*

Born about 551 BC, Confucius was a Chinese teacher, politician, and philosopher who lived during a feudal period in Chinese history. His birthplace was in Zou in the state of Lu, which is near present-day Shandong Province in China. He is credited with having written many of the Chinese classic texts, including the so-called *Five Classics* (Archery, Calligraphy, Computation, Music, and Ritual). His philosophy emphasized personal and governmental ethics and morality, the correctness of social conduct, social justice, and personal integrity.

Confucius's father was in the military and died when Confucius was only three years old. Thus, he was raised by his mother. He married at nineteen and had at least three children. He worked at various jobs in his youth, including as a bookkeeper and government official. Eventually, he rose to the position of Minister of Crime in his hometown. In this position, Confucius tried to implement government reform but was unsuccessful and made many enemies during the process.

As a result, he left his family and hometown to begin a long journey throughout China as an itinerant teacher and philosopher. He returned to Zou when he was sixty-eight and spent his last years teaching about seventy disciples the tenets of the *Five Classics*. After his death, his disciples spread his message throughout Asia. He died about 479 BC at the age of seventy-two. By the second century BC, during China's first Han Dynasty, his ideas became the foundation of the state ideology. Today he is widely considered one of the most influential teachers and philosophers in Chinese history (Creel 1949; Liu 1972).

Chapter 5
SITUATIONAL LEADERSHIP ANALYSIS

Situational models of leadership differ from earlier trait and behavioral models in asserting that no single way of leading works in all situations. Rather, appropriate behavior depends on the circumstances at a given time. Effective managers diagnose the situation, identify the leadership style or behavior that will be most effective, and then determine whether they can implement the required style.

There are a number of instances when Confucius demonstrated his willingness to engage in situational leadership thinking and adapt his leadership style to the changing situation. For example, when he was unable to attain a powerful position in the administration of his hometown, he utilized a little political frame leadership behavior and had his disciples who were trained in his ideologies successfully run for office. And in the *Analects*, a compilation of his ideologies, it tells us that at court when he talked to officials of superior rank he was restrained and formal, while with the lower ranks he was informal and direct.

Again in the *Analects*, it tells us that Confucius was a prototypical situational leader. In a number of places, he is depicted as being "affable yet firm, commanding yet not austere, dignified yet pleasant. He was respectful, though not obsequious." In return, he expected to be treated likewise (Creel 1949, 58).

One of the more remarkable facts about Confucius had to do with his ability to behave situationally. Although being a zealot in his beliefs (structural frame behavior), he was always able to maintain his sense of humor (symbolic frame behavior). He did not often tell jokes, but he saw the humor even in his critics.

One of his contemporaries once remarked with heavy sarcasm, "Great indeed is Confucius! He is vastly learned, and yet he has not made a name for himself in any profession." When Confucius learned of this, he did not defend himself by pointing out that he had gained some considerable repute as a teacher. Instead, he readily acknowledged that this was a grave criticism and jokingly said to his disciples, "Now let me see, what shall I take up? Shall it be charioteering, or archery? I have it; I'll take up charioteering" (Creel 1949, 61).

Confucius was also situational as a teacher. Like every good teacher, he adapted his teaching style to the various learning styles of his students. He sometimes even gave different answers to the same question.

On one occasion, a student asked him whether when he was taught something he should at once put it into practice. Confucius told him, "No," that he should consult with his father and elder brothers first. A little later, another student asked the same question and Confucius told him, "Yes." One of his other students, knowing of the two answers, was puzzled and asked the reason for the difference. Confucius told him, "The [second student] was lacking in zeal, so I urged him on; the first student has more than his own share of energy, so I held him back" (Creel 1949, 79).

THE STRUCTURAL FRAME

Structural frame leaders seek to develop a new model of the relationship of structure, strategy, and environment for their organizations. Strategic planning, extensive preparation, and effecting change are priorities for them. Although Confucius was primarily known as a kind and peaceful man and did not use structural frame behavior as his principal means of leading, he was extremely passionate about his life's mission and did utilize structural frame behavior when appropriate.

For example, when making a choice between following the orders of one's superiors and adhering to his principles, Confucius instructed his disciples to utilize structural frame behavior and stick to their principles. And when asked if he would, like one of the soldiers in the prince's army, ever use structural frame behavior and attack a tiger with his bare hands, he responded that he would prefer the use of another type of structural frame behavior, namely "careful planning."

In true structural frame mode, Confucius expected a great deal from his students. He went so far as to disown one his students because he had assisted the rich and powerful royal family to increase its taxes on the people. Usually, however, he tempered his structural frame behavior with human resource frame behavior and was careful not to go so far as to injure anyone's self-respect. And often he used dry and gentle humor to make his point; thus when one of his students was constantly criticizing another student, he said: "Obviously, Tzu-kung has become quite perfect himself to have time to spare for this; I do not have this much leisure" (Creel 1949, 81).

Structural frame behavior was at the root of how Confucius dealt with his students. He repeatedly said to them: "To study, and when the occasion arises, to put what one has learned into practice—is this not deeply satisfying?" These words, with which the *Analects* open, at once tell us that Confucius was a scholar, and that the aim of his scholarship was practical (Creel 1949, 100).

And like most structural frame practitioners, Confucius was a very practical man. He believed in religion, for example, but considered it in the realm of forces beyond man's control. Thus, rather than arguing about dogma, he was more interested in using religion in making over the intolerable world into a good and gracious world. What nothing could be done about, did not concern him very much. Rather, he was occupied with the very practical problem of how best to utilize one's abilities to act effectively.

Once again, in true structural frame form, Confucius went so far as to develop a laundry list of the nine basic duties of a good prince:

1. To cultivate himself
2. To honor men of worth
3. To be affectionate to his kinsmen
4. To respect great ministers
5. To treat with consideration all officials
6. To take fatherly care of the common people
7. To promote the humble crafts
8. To be hospitable to strangers
9. To be friendly to all neighboring princes (Lui 1972, 165)

These principles might seem modest by today's standards, but in Confucius's time of lawlessness and anarchy, they were rather radical.

Finally, since he was not making progress on his vision to reform the human abuses of China's feudal system, Confucius engaged in even more structural frame behavior and left his hometown. Although nearing the age of sixty, he set off on his pilgrimage determined to find a prince who would give him a real opportunity to put his principles of good government into practice. He was unsuccessful, but after his death his efforts were rewarded when his principles were put into effect by China's first Han Dynasty.

THE HUMAN RESOURCE FRAME

Human resource leaders believe in people and communicate that belief. They are passionate about productivity through people. Like virtually all of the leaders in this study, Confucius made frequent use of human resource frame leadership behavior.

To the young Confucius, the feudal system in China and the human condition that it perpetrated were intolerable. He believed instead that it was "natural" for men to cooperate and promote the common welfare. In his opinion, a ruler's success should be measured by his ability not to win battles and amass wealth and power, but to bring about the welfare and happiness of the people.

Confucius further demonstrated his human resource frame leanings by trying to bring about the reform that he envisioned by a "bloodless revolution." His plan was to eliminate rulers who inherited their thrones in favor of ministers chosen on the basis of merit, and to change the aim of government from aggrandizement of the few to the happiness and welfare of the many, and to do it in a peaceful way.

A man of peace, when Confucius heard the news of a rebellion by some of his followers and a murder in one of China's states, he fasted to the brink of dying to make his point. Twenty-five hundred years later, Mahatma Gandhi used the same tactic in India to make his points. So basically, Confucius believed that true gentlemen are those who act with respect and courtesy toward others as if all were brothers. He taught that nobility depends on the mind and the spirit, not the pedigree, and that "a man's worth depends on what he is, not on what his grandfather was" (Creel 1949, 44).

One last example of the human resource frame being perhaps Confucius' strongest frame involves how he treated the blind. Confucius was careful to make sure to acquaint his blind guests with each of the persons in a room and to inform them of everything about which they might be curious but could not see. Furthermore, he was humane enough to care more for the welfare of human beings than for property. "When his stable burned down, Confucius returning from court asked 'Was anyone hurt?' He did not ask about the horses" (Creel 1949, 60).

THE SYMBOLIC FRAME

In the symbolic frame, the organization is seen as a stage, a theater in which every actor plays certain roles, and the symbolic leader attempts to communicate the right impressions to be the right audiences.

Confucius was hindered somewhat in his use of the symbolic frame in that he was not a very skillful speaker. But he overcame that deficiency by selecting the most articulate of his disciples to speak for him. In addition, he found other means to engage in the symbolic frame. He was, for example, able to coin words and phrases (e.g., the Master, the Way, the Gentleman, Confucianism, and the Silver Rule) that have survived the ages. He also committed to memory the three hundred poems that we know as the *Book of Poetry* for use at appropriate times. And he had a magnetic personality that enabled him to recruit followers in great numbers. He was a powerful "fisher of men" (Creel 1949, 30).

The central conception of the philosophy of Confucius is often expressed in a symbolic frame way. Namely, that of "The Way," which is actualized in the so-called Silver Rule: "Do not do to others what you do not want done to yourself" (Creel 1949, 122).

Confucius engaged in symbolic frame leadership behavior in establishing what he called the "Confucian School," and it was not long before his intelligence, the force of his personality, and his wit made him the recognized "Master" and his students were known as his very loyal "disciples." He taught them to dream of a world in which war and hatred and misery would be replaced by peace, goodwill, and happiness.

In another symbolic frame enactment, Confucius refused offers of government positions because they did not afford him the freedom to implement his vision. One of the lords reproached him for remaining aloof from political appointments, saying, "'Suppose I had a beautiful gem here; should I keep it stored away in a case, or should I seek a good price and sell it?' 'Sell it,' Confucius replied, 'sell it by all means. I, you see, am just waiting for the right price'" (Creel 1949, 38).

Having declared himself to be charged by Heaven with a mission, Confucius engaged in symbolic frame behavior to the point where he was described by one of China's dukes as "the sort of man so intent upon enlightening those eager for knowledge that he forgets to eat, and so happy in doing so that he forgets his sorrows and does not realize that old age in creeping up on him" (Creel 1949, 47).

Confucius's decision to leave his hometown and travel to foreign lands in pursuit of "The Way" was a display of symbolic frame behavior. In doing so, he created a blueprint for those like the knight Don Quixote, who were also seeking their impossible dreams. If he had stayed in Lu, he may have been remembered in history as just another teacher, but as it was, he is remembered as a prophet.

Confucius not only endorsed symbolic frame leadership behavior for himself, but encouraged it among his contemporaries. He believed that heads of states and all officers of the government should provide an example of the highest type of conduct, and he believed that by doing so they would accomplish more than any amount of preaching or punishment could. According to Confucius, it was not a magical compulsion but the power of virtuous example through which rulers influenced their people for good.

In another symbolic frame gesture, rather than constantly demanding blind loyalty from his disciples, Confucius modeled the much more effective lesson of being loyal to *them*. He very seldom criticized them except behind closed doors. His emphasis was not on punishment or coercion, but on persuasion.

Another example of Confucius's prolific use of symbolic frame behavior was his coining of the term "Li" as a guide for discovering "The Way" in which his disciples were to conduct themselves. It meant "good taste." In relation to the individual, the function of Li was to enable one to conduct oneself in a socially acceptable way. Thus, Li differentiated the civilized person from the barbarian who gave immediate and undisciplined vent to his or her feelings.

In advocating for some education for all and undertaking to make educated "gentlemen" out of ambitious commoners, Confucius was not only striking a symbolic blow to monarchies, but also symbolically supporting what we now refer to as "public education"—and doing so five hundred years before the birth of Christ was radical, indeed.

Like Jesus Christ five hundred years later, Confucius used symbolic frame behavior in the form of parables to convey his message. An example was when Confucius and his followers encountered a woman who was visibly anguished.

> "You weep as if you had suffered from great sorrows," one of them said. "It is so," answered the woman. "First my father-in-law was killed by a tiger, then my husband met the same fate; and now death has come to my son!"
> "But why don't you leave this place?"
> "There is no oppressive government here," was her reply.
> Hearing this, the Master turned to his followers and said, "My children, remember this: An oppressive government is fiercer than a tiger." (Liu 1972, 56)

In another parable, it was in answer to a clueless ruler's question about whether he should hand over the government to his favorite concubine that Confucius spoke the following sphinx-like words: "Princes prince; ministers minister; fathers father; sons son." To put these words into modern terms, we would say, "Let a prince be a prince; the minister be a minister; the father a father; and the son, a son" (Liu 1972, 57).

THE POLITICAL FRAME

Leaders operating out of the political frame clarify what they want and what they can get. Political leaders are realists above all. They never let what they want cloud their judgment about what is possible. They assess the distribution of power and interests. They are most interested in "making friends and influencing people."

Confucius's ultimate goal was to dispense with hereditary rulers, but that was out of the question at that point in China's history. So Confucius engaged in some political frame leadership behavior and tried to persuade the rulers to at least outsource their administrative functions to ministers who were virtuous and properly trained in the Confucian tradition. During his lifetime, Confucius was able to cultivate relationships with the ruling bodies whereby he was able to obtain numerous important government appointments for his disciples.

Confucius always urged his disciples to remain true to his principles. But when one of them was found to have collected excessive taxes for his superior, Confucius renounced him but exhibited political frame behavior in allowing him to remain in office, for to remove him at that point in time would have been quixotic. Instead, he tried to move the disciple in the direction he wished him to go while continuing to criticize his excesses.

According to one of his closest disciples, Mencius, the Master's personality was such that it lent itself to a facile use of the political frame. In his view, there were four characteristics of which Confucius was entirely free: he had no foregone conclusions, he was not overpositive, not obstinate, and never saw things from his own point of view alone. Maintaining a middle path was important to him. As Mencius writes in the *Analects*, "Confucius did not go to extremes. To go too far is as bad as to fall short" (Creel 1949, 139).

The fact that no one became particularly alarmed at Confucius's recommendations for public education is a tribute to his effective use of political frame leadership behavior. Unlike his disciple Mencius, who flatly declared that oppressive rulers ought to be put to death, or that there was no inherent difference between a peasant and an emperor, Confucius took a more prudent approach. And, by being somewhat more tactful, he laid the foundation by which it was possible for Mencius and his other disciples to be more dogmatic with impunity a century later.

On the other hand, one of the reasons Confucius was not as successful as he could have been in having his governmental theories adopted was that he was sometimes incapable of acting out of the political frame and making the compromises necessary to place his ideologies into practice. Nevertheless, he recognized this about himself and was self-critical, advising his followers to do the same. "One who is strict with himself, yet indulgent with others avoids resentment" he declared (Creel 1949, 92).

THE MORAL FRAME

As mentioned earlier, the moral frame is my own contribution to situational leadership theory. In my view, the moral frame completes situational leadership theory. Without it, leaders could just as easily use their leadership skills for promoting evil as for promoting good. Leaders operating out of the moral frame are concerned about their obligations and responsibilities to their followers. Moral frame leaders use some type of moral compass to direct their behavior. They practice what has been described as servant leadership and are concerned with those individuals and groups that are marginalized in their organizations and in society. In short, they are concerned about social justice.

Although some say Confucius was not a religious leader, he nonetheless consistently operated from the moral frame. For example, he stoutly refused to take a government appointment that was in fact designed merely to keep him quiet because it would reflect poorly upon his integrity. It would not have been in concert with his repeated assertions that the man of honor did not accept office unless he is able to contribute effectively to good government. "If a man lacks sincerity," he told his students, "I don't know how he can get on, any more than a wagon could without a yoke for attaching the horses" (Creel 1949, 89).

Although Confucius seemed to be a secular humanist rather than a theist, there is no question that he had a moral/ethical standard through which he filtered his leadership behavior. He declined, for example, to have prayers said for him even though he was near death, declaring that he had "done his praying long ago," presumably with deeds rather than words. He looked upon Heaven, however, as the source of his power, which he believed had been entrusted to him with the sacred mission to be a primary shaper of China's culture (Creel 1949, 116).

Unlike other spiritual and religious leaders, Confucius did not preach that virtue would be rewarded in the afterlife. To him, virtue was its own reward, bringing peace of mind and the satisfaction that comes with helping others. "A gentleman, in making his plans, thinks of the Way; he does not think of making a living" (Creel 1949, 117).

KEY IDEAS

As we have seen, whether by intent or instinct, Confucius used the principles of situational leadership theory to his advantage in successfully influencing the lives of millions of Asians and others with his concept of "The Way." It was to what he called his "band of weaklings" that Confucius left his legacy and hopes. Through his effective situational leadership enactments, he did much for them in his own day, kindling in their hearts a flame that has been handed down in an unbroken line to the present generation.

He enamored them with the concept of what it was to be a "gentleman," which henceforth meant a man of learning and gentle bearing rather than a man of noble birth. He called them "knights" and successfully demanded of them the spirit of self-sacrifice and devotion to the common good. As weapons he gave them pens, books, and principles instead of swords. He gave them the mission to go forth boldly and create what Lyndon Johnson later called the "Great Society." Confucius serves as a role model for leaders and aspiring leaders who wish to practice what has been referred to here and elsewhere as servant leadership.

Chapter Six

Jesus Christ

Do unto others as you would have them do unto you.

—The Golden Rule

According to Christian tradition, Jesus Christ was born in Bethlehem to a virgin named Mary. The Christ child was born in a manger in a stable because there was no room at the local inn. Christ grew up in Nazareth but there is little written of his early life other than his visit to the Jewish Temple in Jerusalem when he was about twelve years old.

Christ began his public life at the age of thirty when he left Nazareth and gathered together his twelve apostles. He attracted huge crowds while preaching primarily in Galilee, which is in northern Israel.

Most Christians are familiar with one of Christ's most famous teachings, which took place during the Sermon on the Mount. That day Christ gave his followers the beatitudes and the Lord's Prayer. Christ's teachings centered around what has become known as the Golden Rule—do unto others as you would have them do unto you.

After three years of public ministry, all four Gospels record Christ's triumphal entry into Jerusalem. There, he forcibly removed the money changers from the Temple. While in Jerusalem, he also participated in the Last Supper at which Christians believe he turned bread and wine into his body and blood. This ritual is celebrated daily throughout the world during the sacrifice of the Mass.

Later that night, while praying in the Garden of Gethsemane, Christ was betrayed by the apostle Judas and arrested by Roman soldiers. He was charged with blasphemy for allegedly claiming that he was the Son of God and the King of the Jews.

The familiar story of Christ's death by crucifixion includes his encounter with the Roman prefect Pontius Pilate and his offer to the crowd of the choice between Christ and an insurrectionist named Barabbas. Legend has it that the angry crowd chose to have Barabbas freed and Christ crucified.

According to the Gospels of Matthew, Mark, Luke, and John, Christ died on a cross on Golgotha and was buried by a wealthy Judean named Joseph of Arimathea. On the third day, Christ rose from the dead, thus proving to Christian believers that Christ was truly the Son of God. As a result, Easter Sunday is considered the most significant Christian holiday, even surpassing the importance of Christmas Day.

SITUATIONAL LEADERSHIP ANALYSIS

Situational models of leadership differ from earlier trait and behavioral models in asserting that no single way of leading works in all situations. Rather, appropriate behavior depends on the circumstances at a given time. Effective managers diagnose the situation, identify the leadership style or behavior that will be most effective, and then determine whether they can implement the required style.

The Gospels of Matthew, Mark, Luke, and John leave little doubt that Jesus Christ was a situational leader. A review of Christ's leadership behavior is replete with instances of the use of structural, human resource, symbolic, and even political behavior. Being the consummate teacher, Christ was quite adept at varying his teaching style to the learning style of his "students." He used parables, lectures, stories, and even miracles, depending on the readiness level of his audience.

Perhaps the most notable instance when Christ modeled situational leadership behavior was in speaking to the Pharisees regarding whether the Jewish law would allow them to pay taxes to the Roman emperor. The Pharisees expected a yes-or-no answer, planning to criticize Christ whichever way he answered. However, in a most situational manner, he asked them to identify the head on the coin, and when they identified it as Caesar's, he said, "Then pay Caesar what is due to Caesar, and pay God what is due God" (Matthew 22:21–22).

Another instance among the many in which Christ was situational in his application of leadership behavior was at the Sermon on the Mount when he preached the beatitudes. He knew that there were at least two "situations" among the crowd—those who would immediately understand his message, and those who would need help in doing so. So, in addition to using structural leadership behavior in enumerating the eight beatitudes, Christ used symbolic behavior by cloaking the beatitudes in language that even the most illiterate in the assemblage could understand. Instead of merely telling them to be kind, merciful, and just, he taught them, saying,

Blessed are the poor in spirit, for theirs is the kingdom of heaven.
Blessed are those who mourn, for they shall be comforted.
Blessed are the meek, for they shall inherit the earth.
Blessed are those who hunger and thirst for righteousness, for they shall be filled.
Blessed are the merciful, for they shall obtain mercy.
Blessed are the pure in heart, for they shall see God.
Blessed are the peacemakers, for they shall be called sons of God.
Blessed are those who are persecuted for righteousness' sake, for theirs is the kingdom of heaven. (Matthew 5:2–10)

Lastly, early in his ministry, Christ used situational leadership behavior in refusing the devil's invitation to perform a miracle, while readily agreeing to do so for his mother, Mary. One of the first Gospel stories is the temptation of Christ. The devil tempts Christ three times in the desert. On one occasion, the devil urges the fasting Christ to turn stones into bread to feed himself. Christ refuses to display his power in such a self-serving way. However, he did at the marriage feast of Cana what he would not do in the desert. He did in public what he would not do in private. The devil asked him to change stones into bread to save himself, which he refused to do; his mother asked him to change water into wine to help others, which he immediately did—two different situations calling for two very different leadership behaviors (John 2:10).

THE STRUCTURAL FRAME

Structural frame leaders seek to develop a new model of the relationship of structure, strategy, and environment for their organizations. Strategic planning, extensive preparation, and effecting change are priorities for them. One could argue that Jesus Christ took thirty years to develop a plan to transform the spiritual and personal lives of humankind. By the time he began his public ministry, he had in mind what amounted to a strategic plan for changing the way people would behave and how they would relate to one another.

He had developed a moral code to guide his followers' behavior. As mentioned above, Christ was essentially a teacher. To be effective, he had to make abundant use of structural frame leadership behavior. He used structural leadership behavior in the form of preaching, storytelling, parables, and miracles to make his points and attain his goals. As we shall see, there are myriad examples of Christ effectively utilizing the structural frame.

Even before his public life began, he used structural leadership behavior. In the Gospel story of the "Finding in the Temple," Christ used structural leadership behavior in the form of teaching the temple elders when he was merely twelve years old. In this Gospel episode, Christ accompanies Mary and Joseph to Jerusalem on a pilgrimage. On the day of their return, Christ lingered in the Temple, but Mary and Joseph thought he had gone ahead of them. Mary and Joseph headed back home and after a day of travel realized Christ was missing, so they returned to Jerusalem and found Christ three days later. He was found in the temple in discussion with the elders who were amazed at his learning, especially given his young age. When admonished by Mary, Christ replied, "Why did you seek me? Did you not know that I must be about My Father's business?" (Luke 2:42–51).

Jesus Christ used structural frame leadership behavior very early in his public ministry when he recruited his apostles, most of whom were fishermen, and said very directly to them: "Follow me and I will make you fishers of men" (Matthew 5:19). In those few words, he instructed them to become his followers and revealed to them their primary goal of "saving" humankind. He also indicated that they would have to make sacrifices along the journey. "If anyone desires to come after me, let him deny himself, and take up his cross, and follow me" (Matthew 16:24).

Later, in reciting the beatitudes, he revealed to his disciples exactly who would be their audience and eligible for salvation. "Blessed are the poor in spirit," he said, "for theirs is the kingdom of heaven." He continued, "Blessed are those who mourn, for they shall be comforted. Blessed are the meek, for they shall inherit the earth. Blessed are those who hunger and thirst for righteousness, for they shall be filled. Blessed are the merciful, for they shall obtain mercy. Blessed are the pure in heart, for they shall see God. Blessed are the peacemakers, for they shall be called sons of God." And, finally, "Blessed are those who are persecuted for righteousness' sake, for theirs is the kingdom of heaven" (Matthew 5:3–10).

In typical structural frame form, Christ further instructed his disciples to "take heed that you do not do your charitable deeds before men, to be seen by them." Unless they practiced their service in humility, he declared, they would not be rewarded either on earth or in heaven. In effect, he was instructing them that virtue is its own reward, a message that was frequently reiterated by Christ. And, as we have seen, by Confucius some five hundred years earlier.

When his disciples asked him to teach them how to communicate with their God, Christ again used structural frame behavior and taught them to pray. "In this manner," he said, "pray: Our Father who art in heaven, hallowed be thy name. Thy kingdom come. Thy will be done on earth as it is in heaven" (Matthew 6:9–10). Continuing in his teaching and structural frame mode, Christ instructed his disciples to seek good and avoid evil. "No one can serve two masters; for either he will hate the one and love the other, or else he will be loyal to the one and despise the other. You cannot serve God and mammon," he declared (Matthew 7:1–5).

Another lesson that he taught his followers was to be nonjudgmental. "Judge not," he instructed, "that you be not judged. For with what judgment you judge, you will be judged; and with the same measure you use, it will be measured back to you." In true structural frame form, Christ went on to clarify and reinforce his point. "And why do you look at the speck in your brother's eye, but do not consider the plank in your own eye? Or how can you say to your brother, 'Let me remove the speck out of your eye'; and look, a plank is in your own eye? Hypocrite! First remove the plank from your own eye, and then you will see clearly to remove the speck out of your brother's eye" (Matthew 7:2–6).

Then, since every well-structured organization has its unique set of duties and responsibilities, Christ gave his apostles what amounted to their job descriptions, that is, ministering to the marginalized in society. "Do not go into the way of the Gentiles and do not enter a city of the Samaritans," he told them. "But go rather to the lost sheep of the house of Israel. And as you go, preach, saying, 'The kingdom of heaven is at hand.' Heal the sick, cleanse the lepers, raise the dead, cast out demons. Freely you have received, freely give" (Matthew 10:5–9).

Christ taught his disciples the virtue of justice through the parable of the wheat and the tares (weeds). He said, "The kingdom of heaven is like a man who sowed good seed in his field. But while men slept, his enemy came and sowed tares among the wheat and went his way. But when the grain had sprouted and produced a crop, then the tares also appeared." The servants then asked the owner what they should do. The owner replied, "Let both grow together until the harvest, and at the time of harvest I will say to the reapers, 'First gather together the tares and bind them in bundles to burn them, but gather the wheat into my barn'" (Matthew 13:24–30). Christ explained further that the wheat represented those who do good in their lives, and the tares are those who do evil. Those who do good are rewarded, and those who do evil are punished.

Christ further elucidated on the finality of justice in the parable of the dragnet. He said, "Again, the kingdom of heaven is like a dragnet that was cast into the sea and gathered some of every kind, which when it was full, they drew to shore; and they sat down and gathered the good into vessels, but threw the bad away. So it will be at the end of the age. The angels will come forth, separate the wicked from among the just, and cast them into the furnace of fire. There will be wailing and gnashing of teeth" (Matthew 13:47–50).

And Christ constantly warned of the necessity to always be ready for Judgment Day. He used the parable of the wise and foolish virgins to get his point across:

> Then the kingdom of heaven shall be likened to ten virgins who took their lamps and went out to meet the bridegroom. Now five of them were wise, and five were foolish. Those who were foolish took their lamps and took no oil with them. But the wise took oil in their vessels with their lamps. But while the bridegroom was delayed, they all slumbered and slept. And at midnight a cry was heard, "Behold, the bridegroom is coming; go up to meet him!" Then all those virgins arose and trimmed their lamps. And the foolish said to the wise "Give us some of your oil for our lamps are going out." But the wise answered, saying "No, lest there should not be enough for us and you; but go rather to those who sell and buy for yourselves." And while they went to buy, the bridegroom came, and those who were ready went in with him to the wedding; and the door was shut. Afterward the other virgins came also, saying, "Lord, Lord, open to us!" But he answered and said, "Assuredly, I say to you, I do not know you"; Watch therefore, for you know neither the day nor the hour in which the Son of Man is coming. (Matthew 25:1–13)

Christ used structural frame behavior to set out the rules and regulations regarding marriage and divorce to his disciples. In responding to the Pharisees' question regarding whether it is lawful for a man to divorce his wife for just any reason, Christ replied,

> Have you not read that He who made them at the beginning made them male and female, and said, "For this reason a man shall leave his father and mother and be joined to this wife, and the two shall become one flesh"? So then, they are no longer two but one flesh. Therefore what God has joined together, let no man put asunder. And I say to you, whoever divorces his wife, except for sexual immorality, and marries another, commits adultery; and whoever marries her who is divorced commits adultery. (Matthew 19:4–9)

Christ also used the structural frame to enumerate the requirements for meriting eternal life in heaven, namely keeping the commandments. "If you want to enter into life, keep the commandments," he said. "You shall not murder. You shall not commit adultery. You shall not steal. You shall not bear false witness. Honor your father and your mother. And, you shall love your neighbor as yourself. If you want to be perfect, go, sell what you have and give to the poor, and you will have treasure in heaven" (Matthew 19:17–21).

Perhaps the most famous example of Christ using structural frame leadership behavior is in the Gospel story depicting his cleansing of the temple. The evangelist Matthew writes an account of Christ's visit to the Jewish temple in Jerusalem: "Then Jesus went into the temple of God and drove out all those who bought and sold in the temple, and overturned the tables of the money changers and the seats of those who sold doves. And He said to them, 'It is written, My house shall be called a house of prayer; but you have made it a den of thieves'" (Matthew 21:12–13).

When the scribes tested Christ by asking him which was the greatest commandment, he responded in a very direct, structural frame way: "You shall love the Lord your God with all your heart, with all your soul, and with all your mind. This is the first and great commandment. And the second is like it: You shall love your neighbor as yourself" (Matthew 22:37–40).

Christ sometimes had to use structural leadership behavior in chastising his apostles for some of their transgressions. For example, when he was in the Garden of Gethsemane preparing to face his crucifixion, he told his apostles, "Sit here while I go and pray over there." Then he came to the disciples and found them asleep, and he said to Peter, "What, could you not watch with Me one hour? Watch and pray, lest you enter into temptation. The spirit indeed is willing, but the flesh is weak" (Matthew 26:36–41). And later that same evening, when the Roman soldiers came to arrest Christ, one of his apostles drew his sword and cut off the ear of one of them. Ever the teacher, Christ said to his apostle, "Put your sword in its place, for all who live by the sword will die by the sword" (Matthew 26:52).

In true structural leadership form, Christ used the parable of the light under the basket to teach a lesson on the importance of fully utilizing the gifts and talents that have been inherited. He starts by posing a rhetorical question: "Is a lamp bought to put under a basket or under a bed? Is it not to be set on a lampstand? For there is nothing hidden which will not be revealed, nor has anything been kept secret but that it would come to light. If anyone has ears to hear, let him hear. Take heed what you hear. With the same measure you use, it will be measured to you; and to you who hear, more will be given. For whoever has, to him more will be given; but whoever does not have, even what he has will be taken away from him" (Mark 4:21–25).

Likewise, Christ calls on his followers to practice mercy and forgiveness. He said to his disciples, "It is impossible that no offenses should come, but woe to him through whom they do come! It would be better for him if a millstone were hung around his neck, and he were thrown into the sea, than that he should offend one of these little ones. Take heed to yourselves. If your brother sins against you, rebuke him; and if he repents, forgive him. And if he sins against you seven times a day, and seven times a day returns to you saying, 'I repent,' you shall forgive him seventy times seventy" (Mark 17:1–4).

And in teaching the importance of gratitude, he again uses structural frame behavior in the form of the parable of the ten lepers. The ten lepers asked Christ to have mercy on them and cure them of their affliction. He said to them, "Go show yourselves to the priests." And so they went and were cleansed. But only one of them, a Samaritan, came back to thank Christ. Christ asked the leper, "Were there not ten cleansed? But where are the nine? Were there not any found who returned to give glory to God except this foreigner? Arise, go on your way. Your faith has made thee whole" (Mark 17:14–19).

THE HUMAN RESOURCE FRAME

Human resource leaders believe in people and communicate that belief. They are passionate about productivity through people. One could easily argue that human resource leadership behavior was Christ's primary frame of reference. His primary mission was the salvation of mankind. Thus his life story is replete with instances of his concern for humanity. He was the source of the age-old adage "Greater love has no one than this, than to lay down one's life for his friends" (John 15:13). And of course Christ did just that.

Christ not only had concern for humanity himself but commanded his followers to manifest the same concern. In preaching concern for humanity to his disciples, he said, "You have heard that it was said, 'An eye for an eye and tooth for a tooth.' But I tell you not to resist an evil person. But whoever slaps you on your right cheek, turn the other to him also" (Matthew 5:38–40). The same theme was reiterated by Christ in these words: "You have heard that it was said, 'You shall love your neighbor and hate your enemy.' But I say to you, love your enemies, bless those who curse you, do good to those who hate you, and pray for those who spitefully use you and persecute you" (Matthew 6:43–44).

Christ had such a profound concern for people that he instructed them to "ask, and it will be given to you; seek, and you will find; knock, and it will be opened to you" (Matthew 7:7–8).

Virtually all of Christ's miracles were performed out of love and concern for others. This display of human resource leadership behavior began early in his public life and continued throughout his ministry. One of the first recorded miracles was the cleansing of the leper. "When Christ had come down from the mountain, great multitudes followed Him. And behold, a leper came and worshiped Him, saying, 'Lord, if You are willing, You can make me clean.' Then Jesus put out His hand and touched him saying, 'I am willing; be cleansed,' and immediately his leprosy was cleansed" (Matthew 8:1–3).

Another of his early miracles that demonstrated his concern for others was the familiar story of the water turned to wine at the marriage feast at Cana.

> And when they ran out of wine, the mother of Jesus said to Him, "They have no wine." His mother said to the servants, "Whatever He says to do, do it." Jesus said to them, "Fill the waterpots with water." And they filled them up to the brim. And He said to them, "Draw some out now, and take to the master of the feast." When the master of the feast had tasted the water that was made wine, and did not know where it came from, the master of the feast called the

bridegroom. And he said to him, "Every man at the beginning sets out the good wine, and when the guests have well drunk, then that which is inferior; but you have kept the good wine until now." (John 2:1–10)

Still another miracle that demonstrated Christ's concern for his fellow human beings was the healing of the centurion's servant. "Now when Jesus had entered Capernaum, a centurion came to Him, pleading with Him, saying, 'Lord, my servant is lying at home paralyzed, dreadfully tormented.' And Jesus said to him, 'I will come and heal him.' The centurion answered and said, 'Lord, I am not worthy that You should come under my roof. But only speak a word, and my servant will be healed'" (Matthew 8:5–8).

And then there was the healing of the apostle Peter's mother-in-law. "Now when Jesus had come into Peter's house, He saw his wife's mother lying sick with a fever. And He touched her hand, and the fever left her. Then she arose and served them" (Matthew 8:14–15).

A little later in the Gospels, we learn of Christ saving his apostles while they were out at sea. "Now when He got into a boat, His disciples followed Him. And suddenly a great tempest arose on the sea, so that the boat was covered with the waves. But He was asleep. Then His disciples came to Him and awoke Him, saying, 'Lord, save us! We are perishing!' But He said to them, 'Why are you fearful, O you of little faith?' Then he arose and rebuked the winds and the sea. And there was a great calm" (Matthew 8:23–26). Matthew records further the miracles of the healing of the two demon-possessed men, the healing of the paralytic, and the girl restored to life. These accounts are followed by the healing of the two blind men and the healing of the mute man (Matthew 9:28–38).

All of these miracles manifested Christ's compassion and love for humanity. "And Jesus went about all the cities and villages, teaching in their synagogues, preaching the gospel of the kingdom, and healing every sickness and every disease among the people. But when He saw the multitudes, He was moved with compassion for them, because they were weary and scattered, like sheep having no shepherd" (Matthew 9:35–36). Later Christ said to the people, "Come to Me, all you who labor and are heavy laden, and I will give you rest. Take My yoke upon you and learn from Me, for I am gentle and lowly in heart, and you will find rest for your souls. For My yoke is easy and My burden is light" (Matthew 11:28–30).

One of the more famous Gospel stories that demonstrated Christ's use of human resource behavior is the miracle of the loaves and the fishes.

> And they said to Him, "We have here only five loaves and two fish." He said, "Bring them to Me." Then He commanded the multitudes to sit down on the grass. And He took the five loaves and the two fish, and looking up to heaven, He blessed and broke and gave the loaves to the disciples; and the disciples gave to the multitudes. So they all ate and were filled, and they took up twelve

baskets full of fragments that remained. Now those who had eaten were about five thousand men, besides women and children. (Matthew 14:26–21)

Another beloved Gospel story that is demonstrative of Christ's propensity for human resource behavior is the parable of the good shepherd. "What do you think? If a man has a hundred sheep, and one of them goes astray, does he not leave the ninety-nine and go to the mountains to seek the one that is straying? And if he should find it, assuredly, I say to you, he rejoices more over that sheep than over the ninety-nine that did not go astray" (Matthew 18:10–13). And then there was the parable of the unforgiving servant. "Peter came to Him and said, 'Lord, how often shall my brother sin against me, and I forgive him? Up to seven times?' Jesus said to him, 'I do not say to you, up to seven times, but up to seventy times seven'" (Matthew 18:21–22).

The Gospel writer Mark reinforces Christ's frequent use of human resource leadership behavior by recording such miracles as the healing of the demon-possessed man, the girl restored to health and a woman healed, a blind paralytic man healed at Bethsaida, the healing of Bartimaeus, and the raising of Lazarus. The evangelist Luke tells of Christ's concern for others through the familiar parable of the Good Samaritan.

In this story, Christ once again admonishes his disciples to "love your neighbor as yourself" and tells of a certain man who went down from Jerusalem to Jericho and fell among thieves who stripped him of his clothing, wounded him, and departed, leaving him half dead.

> Now by chance a certain priest came down that road. And when he saw him, he passed by on the other side. Likewise a Levite, when he arrived at the place, came and looked, and passed by on the other side. But a certain Samaritan, as he journeyed, came where he was. And when he saw him, he had compassion on him, and went to him and bandaged his wounds, pouring on oil and wine; and he set him on his own animal, brought him to an inn, and took care of him. So which of these three do you think was neighbor to him who fell among the thieves?" And they said, "He who showed mercy on him." Then Christ said to them, "Go and do likewise." (Luke 10:30–37)

In yet another instance of Christ's penchant for modeling human resource behavior, he tells the story of the lost coin. "Or what woman, having ten silver coins, if she loses one coin, does not light a lamp, sweep the house, and seek diligently until she finds it? And when she has found it, she calls her friends and neighbors together, saying, 'Rejoice with me, for I have found the piece which I lost!' Likewise, I say to you, there is joy in the presence of the angels of God over one sinner who repents" (Luke 15:8–10).

The parable of the prodigal son is another example of how Christ was concerned about all humanity, but especially those who are marginalized and otherwise underserved. Christ said, "A certain man had two sons. And the younger of them said to his father, 'Father, give me the portion of goods that falls to me.' So he divided to them his livelihood. And many days later, the younger son gathered all together, journeyed to a far country, and there wasted his possessions with prodigal living."

After his fortune was gone, the prodigal son decided to return home and ask his father's forgiveness.

> And he arose and came to his father. But when he was still a great way off, his father saw him and had compassion, and ran and fell on his knees and kissed him. And the son said to him, "Father, I have sinned against heaven and in your sight, and am no longer worthy to be called your son." . . . Now his older son was in the field. And as he came and drew near to the house, he heard music and dancing. . . . When he saw his father he said, "Lo, these many years I have been serving you; I never transgressed your commandment at any time; and yet you never gave me a young goat that I might make merry with my friends." . . . The father said, "Son, you are always with me and all I have is yours. It is right that we should make merry and be glad, for your brother was dead and is alive again, and was lost and is found." (Luke 15:11–32)

Another familiar Gospel story reflecting Christ's sensitivity to others is the story of the good thief. "Now one of the criminals hanging there reviled Jesus, saying, 'Are you not the Messiah? Save yourself and us.' The other, however, rebuking him, said in reply, 'Have you no fear of God, for you are subject to the same condemnation? And indeed, we have been condemned justly, for the sentence we received corresponds to our crimes, but this man has done nothing criminal.' Then he said, 'Jesus, remember me when you come into your kingdom.' Jesus replied to him, 'Amen, I say to you, today you will be with me in Paradise'" (Luke 23:39–43).

Lastly, John the Evangelist tells of perhaps Christ's most poignant and compelling words regarding the nature and importance of human resource behavior.

> As the Father loved Me, I also love you. If you keep My commandments, you will abide in My love, just as I have kept My Father's commandments and abide in His love. These things I have spoken to you, that My joy may remain in you, and that your joy may be full. This is My commandment, that you love one another as I have loved you. Greater love has no one than this, than to lay down one's life for his friend. You are My friends if you do whatever I command you. No longer do I call you servants, for a servant does not know what his master is doing; but I have called you friends, for all things that I heard from My Father, I have made known to you. (John 15:9–15)

Chapter 6

THE SYMBOLIC FRAME

In the symbolic frame, the organization is seen as a stage, a theater in which every actor plays certain roles, and the symbolic leader attempts to communicate the right impressions to be the right audiences. This is another frame in which Jesus Christ excelled. His use of stories in the form of parables is a prime example of his prolific use of symbolic frame leadership behavior. The various miracles that he performed were also symbolic in nature.

There are myriad examples of Christ's use of symbolic leadership behavior in the Gospel accounts of his life. Early in his public life, the Gospels tell us that he was tempted by the devil while he was fasting for forty days and forty nights in preparation for his ministry. Knowing that Christ would be hungry by the end of his fasting, the devil said, "If you are the Son of God, command that these stones become bread." Christ's symbolic response was, "It is written, 'Man shall not live by bread alone but by every word that proceeds from the mouth of God'" (Matthew 4:3–4)—the point being that the spiritual or supernatural is oftentimes more important than the material things in life.

Another symbolic gesture on the part of Christ was the parable of the salt and light. In speaking to the multitudes, he said, "You are the salt of the earth, but if the salt loses its flavor, how shall it be seasoned? It is then good for nothing but to be thrown out and trampled under foot by men. You are the light of the world. A city that is set on the hill cannot be hidden. Nor do they light a lamp and put it under a basket, but on a lampstand, and it gives light to all who are in the house. Let your light so shine before men, that they may see your good works, and glorify your Father in heaven" (Matthew 5:13–16).

Christ made the point that immoral thoughts were as evil as immoral deeds by using a parable. "You have heard that it was said to those of old, 'You shall not commit adultery.' But I say to you that whoever looks at a woman to lust for her has already committed adultery with her in his heart. And if your right eye causes you to sin, pluck it out and cast it from you; for it is more profitable for you that one of your members perish, than for your whole body to be cast into hell" (Matthew 5:27–29).

Christ used a parable to warn his followers to beware of duplicitous individuals. "Beware of false prophets who come to you in sheep's clothing, but inwardly they are ravenous wolves," he said. "You will know them by their fruits. Do men gather grapes from thornbushes or figs from thistles? Even so, every good tree bears good fruit, but a bad tree bears bad fruit. . . . Therefore by their fruits you will know them" (Matthew 6:1–3).

Long before the three little pigs found the importance of building one's house on a strong foundation, Christ urged his disciples to build their spiritual lives on a foundation of good works. "Therefore whoever hears these sayings of Mine, and does them, I will liken him to a wise man who built his house on the rock; and the rain descended, the floods came, and the winds blew and beat on that house; and it did not fall, for it was founded on the rock. Now everyone who hears these sayings of Mine, and does not do them, will be like a foolish man who built his house on the sand: and the rain descended, the floods came, and winds blew and beat on that house; and it fell" (Matthew 7:24–28).

The Gospel story of Matthew is another example of Christ using symbolic frame behavior to indicate that all, no matter their role in society or their class, are welcome to join his ministry. After asking Matthew, a tax collector, to join him, the Pharisees asked Jesus why he "ate with tax collectors and sinners." Christ responded by saying, "Those who are well have no need of a physician, but those who are sick? But go and learn what this means: 'I desire mercy and not sacrifice.' For I did not come to call the righteous, but sinners, to repentance" (Matthew 9:12–13).

Oftentimes, instead of answering the question of whether he was the Son of God directly, Christ responded in symbolic terms. On one occasion, John the Baptist's disciples asked him, "Are you the Coming One, or do we look for another?" Christ said to them, "Go and tell John the things which you hear and see: The blind receive their sight and the lame walk; the lepers are cleansed and the deaf hear; the dead are raised up and the poor have the gospel preached to them" (Matthew 11:3–5).

Christ taught the value of loyalty and teamwork through the parable of a house divided against itself. Despite both Christ and the Pharisees being Jewish preachers, the Pharisees oftentimes challenged Christ. In one instance in the Gospels, they accused him of performing miracles in the name of Beelzebub, or the devil. But Christ knew their real thoughts and said to them, "Every kingdom divided against itself will not stand. And if Satan casts out Satan, he is divided against himself. How then will his kingdom stand? . . . He who is not with Me is against Me, and he who does not gather with Me scatters abroad" (Matthew 12:25–26, 30).

Even though Christ intended his message for all humankind, he warned his followers in symbolic terms that many would not heed his word. In the parable of the sower, Christ said to the multitude, "Behold, a sower went out to sow. And as he sowed, some seed fell by the wayside; and the birds came and devoured them. Some fell on stony places, where they did not have much earth; and they immediately sprang up because they had no depth of earth. But when the sun was up they were scorched, and because they had no root they withered away. And some fell among thorns, and the thorns sprang up and choked them. But others fell on good ground and yielded a crop: some a hundredfold, some sixty, some thirty. He who has ears to hear, let him hear!" (Matthew 13:1–9).

Christ preached that everyone, even the lowliest, is born with gifts and talents. In the familiar parable of the mustard seed, Christ once again makes his point in a symbolic way. "The kingdom of heaven is like a mustard seed, which a man took and sowed in his field, which indeed is the least of all the seeds; but when it is grown it is greater than the herbs and becomes a tree, so that the birds of the air come and nest in its branches" (Matthew 13:31–32).

In yet another symbolic frame gesture, Christ observes that prophets and other leaders are rarely appreciated immediately. It is usually left to history to determine their effectiveness. He said, "A prophet is not without honor except in his own country and in his own house" (Matthew 13:57). The obvious message to leaders is not to expect credit for their achievements in the short term; better to be intrinsically motivated and let history be the judge.

Instead of simply asserting his claim to be the Son of God, Christ performed many miracles to indicate symbolically that he was a special leader and, in his followers' view, their Savior.

One such miracle was the familiar Gospel story of Christ walking on water. "Immediately Jesus made His disciples get into the boat and go before Him to the other side, while He sent the multitudes away. . . . But the boat was now in the middle of the seas, tossed by the waves, for the wind was contrary. . . . And they cried out in fear. Now . . . Jesus went to them, walking on the seas. And when the disciples saw Him walking on the sea, they were troubled, saying, 'It is a ghost!' But immediately Jesus spoke to them, saying, 'Be of good cheer! It is I: don't be afraid.'" Christ asked Peter to come to him in the water, and Peter walked on the water to go to Jesus. "But when he saw that the wind was boisterous, he was afraid: and beginning to sink he cried out, saying, 'Lord, save me!' And immediately Jesus stretched out His hand and caught him, and said to him, 'O you of little faith, why did you doubt?'" (Matthew 14:22–31).

Christ warned his followers in symbolic frame terms that they should beware of "false prophets," or those who stretch and manipulate the facts in symbolic terms. He likened these individuals to blind persons. "They are blind leaders of the blind. And if the blind leads the blind, both will fall into a ditch" (Matthew 15:14).

Christ even established his church and named its earthly leader by using symbolic leadership behavior. He said to the apostle Simon Peter, whose name meant "rock" in Hebrew, "Blessed are you, Simon Bar-Jonah, for flesh and blood has not revealed this to you, but My Father who is in heaven. And I also say to you that you are Peter, and on this rock I will build My church, and the gates of Hades shall not prevail against it. And I will give you the keys of the kingdom of heaven, and whatever you bind on earth will be bound in heaven and whatever you loose on earth will be loosed in heaven" (Matthew 16:17–19).

The miracle of the Transfiguration is another instance of Christ using symbolic frame behavior to demonstrate his divine nature to his disciples.

"Now after six days Jesus took Peter, James, and John his brother, brought them up on a high mountain by themselves, and was transfigured before them. His face shone like the sun, and His clothes became as white as the light. Now as they came down from the mountain, Jesus commanded them, saying, 'Tell the vision to no one until the Son of Man is risen from the dead'" (Mark 9.2).

For those of his followers who were fortunate enough to be materially successful, Christ had the following symbolic frame advice for them: "Assuredly, I say to you that it is hard for a rich man to enter the kingdom of heaven. And again I say to you, it is easier for a camel to go through the eye of a needle than for a rich man to enter the kingdom of God." He also reminded us that "many who are first will be last and the last first. For many are called and few are chosen" (Matthew 19:23–30).

Christ beseeched his followers to seek good and avoid evil and to do so constantly, in that one never knows when life will come to an end. His disciples, of course, believe that a good life will be rewarded, if not in this life, then in the next. But Christ warns, "But of that day and hour no one knows, no, not even the angels of heaven, but My Father only. . . . Therefore you also be ready, for the Son of Man is coming at an hour when you do not expect Him" (Matthew 24:36–44).

Christ further espoused doing good over evil when he said, "And if your hand makes you sin, cut it off. It is better for you to enter into life maimed, than having two hands to go to hell, into the fire that shall never be quenched" (Mark 9:43).

Christ also preached social justice and urged his followers to treat everyone with human dignity. He once again used symbolism to get this point across to his disciples.

> Then the King will say to those on His right hand, "Come, you blessed of My Father, inherit the kingdom prepared for you from the foundation of the world: for I was hungry and you gave Me food; I was thirsty and you gave Me drink; I was a stranger and you took Me in. I was naked and you clothed Me; I was sick and you visited Me; I was in prison and you came to Me." And the righteous will answer Him, saying, "Lord, when did we see You hungry and feed You, or thirsty and give You drink? When did we see You a stranger and take You in, or naked and clothe You? Or when did we see You sick, or in prison, and come to You?" And the King will answer and say to them, "Assuredly, I say to you, in as much as you did it to one of the least of these My brethren, you did it to Me." (Matthew 25:34–40)

In perhaps Christ's most memorable symbolic frame leadership gesture, he left his followers with a symbol to remember him by after he had gone. In the Gospel story of the Last Supper, Christ took bread, blessed it, broke it, and gave it to the disciples and said, "Take, eat; this is My body." Then he took the cup, gave thanks, and gave it to them, saying, "Drink from it, all of you. For this is My blood of the new covenant, which is shed for many for the remission of sins. Do this in remembrance of Me" (Matthew 26:26–29). These words are repeated even today at every Roman Catholic Mass and similar services in other Christian rites.

Another value that Christ promoted symbolically was that of generosity or philanthropy. However, he also cautioned against being boastful about one's own generosity as opposed to another's in the parable of the widow's two mites. "Now Jesus sat opposite the treasury and saw how the people put money into the treasury. And many who were rich put in much. Then one poor widow came and threw in two mites, which make a quadrans. So He called His disciples to Him and said to them, 'Assuredly, I say to you that this poor widow has put in more than all those who have given to the treasury; for they all put in out of their abundance, but she out of her poverty put in all that she had, her whole livelihood'" (Mark 12:41–44).

Christ also taught the value of sacrifice in a symbolic frame way. "Then He said to them all, 'If anyone desire to come after Me, let him deny himself, and take up his cross daily, and follow Me. For whoever desires to save his life will lose it, but whoever loses his life for My sake will save it. For what advantage is it to a man if he gains the whole world, and is himself destroyed or lost?'" (Luke 9:23–25).

In the parable of the Pharisee and the tax collector, Christ taught his followers the virtue of humility.

> Also He spoke this parable to some who trusted in themselves that they were righteous, and despised others: "Two men went up to the temple to pray, one a Pharisee and other a tax collector. The Pharisee stood and prayed thus with himself, 'God, I thank You that I am not like other men—extortioners, unjust, adulterers, or even as this tax collector. I fast twice a week; I give tithes of all that I possess.' And the tax collector, standing afar off, would not so much as raise his eyes to heaven, but beat his breast, saying, 'God be merciful to me a sinner!' I tell you, this man went down to his house justified rather than the other; for everyone who exalts himself will be abased, and he who humbles himself will be exalted." (Luke 18:9–14)

Lastly, Christ used symbolic frame language to foretell his resurrection and death. "Jesus answered and said to them, 'Destroy this temple, and in three days I will raise it up'" (John 3:19). Later Christ likened himself to bread in saying, "I am the bread of life. He who comes to Me shall never hunger, and he who believes in Me shall never thirst" (John 6:35). Next, Christ made a point of the need to seek the truth by saying, "And you shall know the truth, and the truth shall set you free" (John 8:33), a quote often used by Martin Luther King Jr. As these many examples indicate, Jesus Christ made frequent use of symbolic frame leadership behavior.

THE POLITICAL FRAME

Leaders operating out of the political frame clarify what they want and what they can get. Political leaders are realists above all. They never let what they want cloud their judgment about what is possible. They assess the distribution of power and interests. They are most interested in "making friends and influencing people."

Although Jesus Christ did not utilize the political frame as often as the others, there is ample evidence in the Gospels that he used this type of leadership behavior when the situation demanded it. He warned his disciples that he was sending them out into a political world and suggested ways in which they could survive it. "Behold, I send you out as sheep in the midst of wolves. Therefore be wise as serpents and harmless as doves," he counseled them (Matthew 10:16).

Then he identified for them the traits of the "serpents" that they would encounter. He said, "Either make the tree good and its fruit good, or else make the tree bad and its fruit bad; for a tree is known by its fruit. Brood of vipers! How can you, being evil, speak good things? For out of the abundance of the heart the mouth speaks. But I say to you that for every idle word men may speak, they will give account of it in the day of judgment. For by your words you will be justified, and by your words you will be condemned" (Matthew 12:33–37).

Much of Christ's political frame behavior was aimed at the Pharisees and other religious leaders who were continually testing him. "Then some of the scribes and Pharisees answered, saying, 'Teacher, we want to see a sign from You.' But He answered and said to them, 'An evil and adulterous generation seeks after a sign, and no sign will be given to it except the sign of the prophet Jonah. For as Jonah was three days and three nights in the belly of the great fish, so will the Son of Man be three days and three nights in the heart of the earth" (Matthew 12:38–40). In other words, the Pharisees would have to wait for their "sign" until Christ rose from the dead.

Christ utilized the political frame once again in dealing with these religious officials.

> Now when He came into the temple, the chief priests and the elders of the people confronted Him as He was teaching, and said, "By what authority are You doing these things? And who gave You this authority?" But Jesus answered and said to them, "I also will ask you one thing, which if you tell Me, I likewise will tell you by what authority I do these things. The baptism of John, where was it from? From heaven or from men?" And they reasoned among themselves, saying, "If we say, 'From heaven,' He will say to us, 'Why then did you not believe him?' But if we say, 'From men,' we fear the multitude, for all count John as a prophet." So they answered Jesus and said, "we do not

know." And He said to them, "Neither will I tell you by what authority I do these things." (Matthew 21:23–27)

Thus, those setting the trap found themselves trapped by Christ.

In perhaps Christ's most famous use of political frame leadership behavior, the Pharisees were once again trying to trap him.

> Then the Pharisees went and plotted how they might entangle Him in His talk. And they sent to Him their disciples with the Herodians, saying "Teacher, we know that You are true, and teach the way of God in truth; nor do you care about anyone, for You do not regard the person of men. Tell us, therefore, what do You think? Is it lawful to pay taxes to Caesar, or not?" But Jesus perceived their wickedness, and said, "Why do you test Me, you hypocrites? Show Me the tax money." So they brought Him a denarius. And He said to them, "Whose image and inscription is this?" They said to Him, "Caesar's." And He said to them, "Render therefore to Caesar the things that are Caesar's, and to God the things that are God's." When they had heard these words, they marveled, and left Him and went on their way. (Matthew 22:15–22)

Game, set, match, Jesus Christ!

Christ then showed his disciples how to engage in political frame behavior when appropriate. "Then Jesus spoke to the multitudes and to His disciples, saying: 'The scribes and the Pharisees sit in Moses' seat. Therefore whatever they tell you to observe, that observe and do, but do not do according to their works; for they say, and do not do'" (Matthew 23:1–3). Christ, in effect, advised his disciples to obey the law, but not to behave like the scribes and Pharisees—the age-old adage of doing what I say, not what I do.

Christ also warned his disciples about the misuse of political frame enactments in the form of hypocrisy and lies. He said to the multitude, "Beware of the leaven of the Pharisees, which is hypocrisy. For there is nothing covered that will not be revealed, nor hidden that will not be known. Therefore whatever you have spoken in the dark will be heard in the light, and what you have spoken in the ear in inner rooms will be proclaimed on the housetops" (Luke 12:1–3).

In a typical political frame gesture, Christ advised his followers to make peace with their adversaries whenever possible. "Yes, and why, even of yourselves, do you not judge what is right? When you go with your adversary to the magistrate, make every effort along the way to settle with him, lest he drag you to the judge, the judge deliver you to the officer, and the officer throw you into prison" (Luke 12:57–58).

Christ found a need to engage in political frame behavior on the last days of his earthly life. After he had been arrested in the Garden of Gethsemane, the Jewish Sanhedrin questioned him about whether he was really the Son of God, hoping to convict him of blasphemy if he said he was. However, in true political frame form, Christ deflected the question right back at them and induced them into making the claim rather than himself having to do so. "As soon as it was day, the elders of the people, both chief priests and scribes came together and led Him into their council, saying, 'If You are the Christ, tell us.' But He said to them, 'If I tell you, you will by no means believe. And if I also ask you, you will by no means answer Me or let Me go. Hereafter the Son of Man will sit on the right hand of the power of God.' Then they all said, 'Are You then the Son of God?' And He said to them, '*You* rightly say that I am'" (Luke 22:66–70). Of course, even though Christ outwitted them, they crucified him anyway.

THE MORAL FRAME

As mentioned earlier, the moral frame is my own contribution to situational leadership theory. In my view, the moral frame completes situational leadership theory. Without it, leaders could just as easily use their leadership skills for promoting evil as for promoting good. Leaders operating out of the moral frame are concerned about their obligations and responsibilities to their followers. Moral frame leaders use some type of moral compass to direct their behavior. They practice what has been described as servant leadership and are concerned with those individuals and groups that are marginalized in their organizations and in society. In short, they are concerned about social justice.

Being a Jew, Christ made great use of the moral and ethical values passed along from his ancestors in the Old Testament. Certainly, the prophets and moral men and women who preceded him were practitioners of moral frame leadership behavior, but it could be argued that such behavior was additionally codified by Jesus Christ and perpetuated by his followers who called themselves Christians. At any rate, it is abundantly clear from the Gospel stories cited here that Jesus Christ viewed his leadership behavior through a moral lens and was vitally concerned with personal integrity and social justice. His most fundamental message was the moral frame charge to "do unto others what you would have them do unto you."

KEY IDEAS

Jesus Christ was a prototypical situational leader. As perhaps the most effective leader in history, he operated out of all five of the leadership frames suggested here. He engaged in structural frame leadership behavior by clearly stating what he expected of his followers—that they would love him, keep his commandments, and love their neighbors as they loved themselves. Basic to his mission was his love for humankind, a human resource leadership trait.

He proved his love for humankind by making the ultimate sacrifice and giving up his life for them.

Christ promulgated his message in the form of parables and stories, a distinctly symbolic frame leadership behavior. He also performed miracles to verify his message, which is another indication of his use of symbolic behavior. He even engaged in political leadership behavior when appropriate. His classic advice to give God what is God's and Caesar what is Caesar's is the epitome of an effective use of the political leadership frame.

Finally, his entire public life was dedicated to establishing a moral code by which his followers could live. So it could be accurately asserted that he made prolific use of moral frame leadership behavior. In fact, it could be argued that the moral frame was Christ's foundational frame. Suffice it to say, Christians and non-Christians alike would do well to model their leadership behavior after that of Jesus Christ.

Chapter Seven

Muhammad

Muhammad was born around 570 in the Arabian city of Mecca. He is thought of by Muslims as the last prophet sent by God (Allah) to lead mankind to salvation. He became an orphan at an early age and was raised by his uncle. He worked primarily as a merchant until he reached the age of forty, when while on a retreat in the mountains he was visited by the angel Gabriel and received a revelation from Allah.

Like most religious leaders, Muhammad had few followers at first and was met with hostility by the Meccan tribes. But in 622, Muhammad led his followers from Mecca to Medina in what became known as the Hijra. From his headquarters in Medina, Muhammad led his followers into battle against the Meccans at Badr, Uhud, and the Battle of the Trench. In this last battle, he finally gained control over the city of Mecca. After the battle of the Trench, the Meccan tribe of Quraysh and the Muslim community in Medina signed a ten-year truce called the Treaty of Hudaybiyyah.

In 632, a few months after returning to Medina, Muhammad went on a Farewell Pilgrimage, but soon fell ill and died. By the time of his death, most of the Arabian Peninsula had converted to Islam, and he united Arabia into a single political state. The revelations that Muhammad received from Allah were compiled into the Muslim bible called the Quran. It is estimated that well over a billion people now belong to the Muslim faith, second only to the Christian faith; and of the major religions, it is the fastest growing (Armstrong 1992).

SITUATIONAL LEADERSHIP ANALYSIS

Situational models of leadership differ from earlier trait and behavioral models in asserting that no single way of leading works in all situations. Rather, appropriate behavior depends on the circumstances at a given time. Effective managers diagnose the situation, identify the leadership style or behavior that will be most effective, and then determine whether they can implement the required style.

There is no denying that Muhammad was a gifted leader. He was a spiritual and political leader as well as a military leader. Thus, out of necessity, he needed to utilize the full spectrum of leadership enactments to be effective in all his spheres of influence. We will see him playing with children, having marital problems, weeping bitterly when a friend dies, and showing off his new baby son like any other proud father. We will also see him enthusiastically spreading the word of Allah to his followers, laying down rules, regulations, and laws regarding how they should conduct their daily lives, and leading them into battle in what he deemed to be just wars, all the while moving in and out the various leadership frames.

At first, Muhammad insisted that he had no political function so he utilized the political frame sparingly. But events that could not have been foreseen thrust him into the political arena where he had to utilize the political frame more frequently in order to succeed. Once he and his followers were invited to emigrate from Mecca to Medina from where he would ultimately unify all of Arabia and where intratribal warfare would no longer be the norm, the effective use of political frame leadership behavior would be a requisite for success.

Later in his life, Muhammad was forced to utilize structural frame leadership behavior in the form of coercion to reach his objectives. Rarely is a radical social and/or political change achieved without some form of bloodshed, and because Muhammad lived during a time when anarchy and tribal warfare prevailed, he would be forced to adapt his leadership behavior to the *situation*. Furthermore, since he had no detailed picture of how he would reform the idolatry of the Arab people and had no monotheistic tradition to lean on, he had to adapt to each situation as it arose.

To add to the need for flexibility with regard to Muhammad's use of the five leadership frames was the fact that his conception of his mission appears to have changed from a limited to a broader one, especially after the Battle of the Trench in 627. Since the earlier victory at Badr, he had begun to see that Arab unity was no longer an impossibility. Now his victories had impressed the Bedouin tribes, many of which were now ready to abandon the worship of many gods and enter an alliance with the people of Medina. Muhammad now believed that Allah had sent him as a prophet to *all* the Arabs, and thus he would have to adapt his leadership style even further (Armstrong 1992).

THE STRUCTURAL FRAME

Structural frame leaders seek to develop a new model of the relationship of structure, strategy, and environment for their organizations. Strategic planning, extensive preparation, and effecting change are priorities for them. Muhammad took forty years to develop a plan to transform the spiritual and personal lives of humankind. By the time he began his public ministry, he had in mind, albeit incomplete, what amounted to a strategic plan for changing the way people would behave and how they would relate to one another. His strategic plan contained the five essential pillars of Islam: (1) Almsgiving, (2) Declaration of Faith, (3) Daily Prayer, (4) Fasting in the Month of Ramadan, and (5) A Pilgrimage to Mecca.

Even in early life, Muhammad was assertive in his views. When asked to swear by the goddesses of his people, he would answer truthfully. "Do not ask me (to swear by goddesses)," he protested, "for nothing is more hateful than those two (goddesses)." Instead he swore by Allah alone (Armstrong 1992, 78).

Muhammad took a very structural frame approach in sharing his belief that there was but one God, Allah. According to Muhammad, all lower order creatures acknowledge God and bow before Him, recognizing Him as their first cause, the source of their being without which they could not continue to exist. Likewise, he demanded that his followers bow before God in ritual prayer twice a day. The act of essential surrender to Allah was expected. In fact, the meaning of the word "Muslim" is "one who surrenders." Muhammad reasoned that this act of surrender was particularly required of mankind because man alone has the freedom to make a voluntary choice of Islam (surrender) and consciously fashion his life according to Muslim traditions (Armstrong 1992).

In the early days of his evangelizing, Muhammad made frequent use of the structural frame leadership behavior. But some of it backfired. When he forbade his early followers to worship the pagan idols of Rome, he discovered that he lost many of them and that his strict adherence to the Quran was about to split the tribe. As a result, some of the tribe followed the dissenters to the outskirts of Mecca and attacked them. The dissenters fought back, shedding the first blood for Islam. The pagan gods were regarded as the guardians of the state. The Arabs believed that if their cult was neglected, the gods would withdraw their protection.

Thus, the worship of one god was a sea change for them. It seems as though in Muhammad's mind, converting them would require a strong application of structural frame leadership behavior. As we shall see, he later tempered his use of the structural frame with the use of the human resource and political frames.

Muhammad engaged in more structural frame behavior in asking the Muslims in Medina to make a pledge of war (jihad or Holy War), which required them to defend their Muslim counterparts even if it cost them physical suffering. In other words, as with the practitioners of a number of other religions, Muslims were expected to be martyrs for their faith, if it became necessary.

Muhammad continued to employ a more strident version of structural frame leadership behavior by engaging in a general strategy of encouraging attacks against the Meccan caravans as they crossed the desert near Medina. In 623, Muhammad himself led such a raid. However, the Meccan caravan successfully evaded the Muslims and happily no blood was shed.

Over time, Muhammad became a more effective military tactician. He made certain, for example, that his troops were well trained, and often employed them in creative ways. In one famous battle (The Battle of the Trench), he had his troops gather in the crops from the outlying areas so that the besieging army would have no additional food supplies. In addition, he had his troops build an enormous trench around the oasis, and won the battle decisively because the Meccans were not prepared to deal with this innovative tactic.

Later, Muhammad combined a much less extreme form of structural frame behavior with political frame behavior and entered into a treaty between the Arab and Jewish tribes of Medina. The plan was for the various tribes that shared the oasis to put aside their differences and form a new ummah (community). From then on, the ummah transcended the tribe loyalties. This was unprecedented in Muhammad's era where for centuries the tribes were paramount.

When Muhammad and an army of ten thousand converts finally besieged Mecca and occupied the city in a bloodless takeover, he engaged in a combination of structural and symbolic frame behavior and smashed each of the 360 idols that surrounded the city. Eventually Islam would forbid the use of all imagery in its worship, because it could serve to distract from the purely spiritual realm and the exclusive adoration of Allah. Within a few years, paganism was a thing of the past in Mecca, and most of the pagans converted to Islam (Armstrong 1992).

THE HUMAN RESOURCE FRAME

Human resource frame leaders believe in people and communicate that belief. They are passionate about productivity through people. One could argue that human resource leadership behavior was one of Muhammad's primary frames of reference. We know, for example, that he made almsgiving one of the five pillars of Islam. And the early message of the Quran is clear and simple: "It is wrong to stockpile wealth to build a personal fortune, but good to give alms and distribute the wealth of society" (Armstrong 1992, 92).

Possibly as a result of being orphaned at an early age, Muhammad remained concerned for the plight and treatment of orphans throughout his life. As ironic as it might seem, considering the culture at the time he lived, Muhammad even engaged in human resource frame behavior where women were involved. Previous to Islam, most Meccans and other Arabs thought very little of the female gender. But Muhammad seemed genuinely comfortable in the presence of women and was concerned for their welfare. In his later years, his gentlemanliness and apparent leniency with the women in his life perplexed some of his closest followers.

Muhammad demonstrated his human resource frame side in contributing a large portion of his family income to the poor and encouraged his own family to live very frugally. He also loved children. He was very demonstrative in hugging and kissing them and enthusiastically joining in their games.

Muhammad even displayed his tendency toward human resource frame behavior on the battlefield. For example, the Muslims were justly jubilant with their victory in the Battle of Badr, but when his troops began to execute their prisoners, which was an Arab tradition, Muhammad immediately put a stop to it. Regarding prisoners of war, Muhammad instructed his troops: "You must feed them as you feed yourselves, and clothe them as you clothe yourselves" (Armstrong 1992, 176).

In one final demonstration of Muhammad's use of the human resource frame, we refer to a tradition that recalls an occasion when Muhammad passed sentence on a poor man who had committed a minor crime. For his penance he was told to give alms to the poor. The man replied that he had neither food nor goods to give away. Just at that moment a large basket of dates was delivered into the mosque as a gift to Muhammad. "Here you are," Muhammad said, and told the man to distribute the dates among the poor. The criminal replied that he honestly did not know anyone in the settlement who was worse off than himself. Muhammad laughed and told him that eating the dates himself would be his penance (Armstrong 1992, 231).

THE SYMBOLIC FRAME

In the symbolic frame, the organization is seen as a stage, a theater in which every actor plays certain roles, and the symbolic leader attempts to communicate the right impressions to be the right audiences. One of the reasons why the leaders profiled here have had such a profound and enduring influence on societies across the globe is that they have uniformly been successful in utilizing the symbolic frame. And Muhammad is no exception to the rule.

Muhammad had early exposure to the value of symbolic frame leadership. His guardians (he was an orphan) were active members of the League of the Virtuous whose members swore that they would always take the side of the wronged and oppressed—similar to the image of the Knights of the Round Table. The young Muhammad was said to have been present at a number of the League's meetings and spoke highly of their chivalrous image, which he strove to imitate later in life.

When he began his public life at age forty, Muhammad utilized symbolic frame leadership behavior in the form of the many spiritual retreats in which he took part and later conducted. He had begun to spend more time in solitude, devoting himself to the worship of Allah. During these retreats he also took time to distribute food to the poor. He used these symbolic frame enactments to inspire his early followers to later make prayer and almsgiving essential elements of Islam. In other words, he led by example.

Of course, the familiar story of the appearance of the angel Gabriel was a symbolic frame gesture. As the story goes, Gabriel appeared to Muhammad and spoke the first words of the Quran:

> Recite: in the name of the Lord who created!
> He created man from a clot of blood.
> Recite: and thy Lord is the Most Bountiful.
> He who hath taught by the pen,
> Taught man what he knew not. (Armstrong 1992, 83)

The Quran was itself a symbolic frame enactment meant to inspire Muhammad's followers. The Jews and Christians had their books of spiritual revelations and so would the Muslims. The revelation that Muhammad had started to recite under divine inspiration on Mount Hira was the basis for the Arabic Bible—the Quran. In effect, he was bringing God's essential message to his disciples: men and women must look after the disadvantaged people of the tribe.

Another form of symbolic frame behavior was the way Muhammad lived his life. He always lived a simple and frugal life, even when he became the most powerful person in Arabia. He disliked luxury and there was often little to eat in his household. He never had more than one set of clothes at a time and when he received gifts or booty from battle, he gave them to the poor. He constantly preached to his followers that the poor would enter the Kingdom of Heaven before the rich, and then in true symbolic frame form, went about modeling this desired behavior.

The emigration from Mecca to Medina (the Hijra) was another instance of Muhammad engaging in symbolic frame leadership behavior. It was not merely a geographical change. The Muslims in Mecca were about to abandon the Jewish tribe and their traditions and accept the permanent protection of a

Muslim tribe with whom they were not blood related. It was unprecedented and was as offensive to Arab sensibilities as the earlier symbolic act—the denigration of the pagan goddesses.

In a related symbolic gesture, Muhammad and his close companion, Abu Bakr, remained behind until everyone else had made the Hijra to Medina. When it was finally time to leave, Abu Bakr wanted to give the best camel to Muhammad, but Muhammad insisted on paying for it himself. This would be his personal hijra and gift to Allah, so it was important that he made the event entirely his own (Armstrong 1992).

Perhaps the two most familiar displays of symbolic frame behavior attributed to Muhammad were the concept of the so-called Holy War (jihad) and the Muslim tradition of praying while facing Mecca rather than Jerusalem. Praying while facing Mecca was symbolic because it marked the advent of Muhammad's turning away from Judaism and the Jewish theological traditions and adopting a more Arabian and Islamic outlook. As far as the jihad (struggling/striving/crusade) was concerned, it was a way of defining, through the Quran, what would constitute a just war if no peaceful alternative to preserving Islam could be found—very similar to the justification of the Christian Crusades of the Middle Ages (Armstrong 1992).

THE POLITICAL FRAME

Leaders operating out of the political frame clarify what they want and what they can get. Political leaders are realists above all. They never let what they want cloud their judgment about what is possible. They assess the distribution of power and interests. They are most interested in "making friends and influencing people." Although the conventional wisdom, at least among non-Muslims, might be that Muhammad was somewhat rigid and thus stuck in the structural frame, we shall see that he often engaged in the political frame when appropriate.

Even before he began his public life, Muhammad had gained a reputation for fairness in his tribe. Oftentimes, he settled tribal disputes by using political frame behavior to arrive at an acceptable compromise. For example, there is the story about when he was asked to settle a dispute over setting the sacred Black Stone back into position in the place of pagan worship after it had been repaired. Muhammad asked the tribal officials to bring him a cloak. He then laid the stone in the middle of the cloak and then had a representative of each clan take hold of an edge so they could lift it back into place together.

Although Islam claims to be the one true religion worshiping the one true God, Muhammad adhered to the Arab tradition of using political frame behavior in accommodating all faiths. As is still the case today, Muslims had a reputation of being able to coexist with people of other faiths. For example, the Islamic empire was able to play peaceful host to Christians and Jews for centuries. On the other hand, some Christian countries in the West have historically had a problem with tolerating Jews and Muslims.

In fact, the Quran itself was seen by Muhammad, its author, not so much as revelatory, but as a *reminder* of things that everyone already knew. Frequently the Quran introduces a new topic with the words, "Has thou not seen?" or "Have you not considered," the implication being that Christians and Jews are also welcome (Armstrong 1992, 95).

When Muhammad first began his public life, he had to be sure to be sensitive to the Arabs' pagan roots. So he applied some political frame behavior and wrote two verses of the Quran that were interpreted as being accommodating to the three pagan goddesses. They became known as the Satanic Verses, because they were thought to be inspired not by Allah, but by the devil. Later Muhammad revised the two verses to make them more acceptable. Nevertheless, he seemed to have given a place to the three goddesses without compromising his monotheistic vision with the words:

> Have you considered al-Lat and al-Uzza and Manat (the three goddesses) the third, the other? These are the exalted birds whose intercession is approved. (Armstrong 1992, 114)

In addition to his apparent concessions to the pagans, Muhammad was also sensitive to the feelings of the Jews. Thus, he used political frame leadership behavior in associating the new Meccan faith (Islam) to that of the "People of the Bible (Jews)." For example, he included some important Jewish practices in the Islamic rituals. Above all, Muhammad had Muslims pray facing Jerusalem (later changed to Mecca), as the Jews and Christians did. And Muhammad's so-called Night Journey to Jerusalem had demonstrated that this ancient holy city was central to the Muslims also.

He also instructed his assistant to schedule special meetings of the Muslims on Friday afternoons, at the time when the Jews would be preparing for their Sabbath; this linked the new services with the Jewish festival, while at the same time keeping a tactful distance. In still another instance of his use of political frame behavior, when his followers complained of the frequent number of times they had to pray each day, Muhammad kept going back to Allah until he got the number reduced to a more tolerable five times a day.

In order to keep the Jews and Christians satisfied and unthreatened, Muhammad utilized political frame leadership behavior and wrote in the Quran:

> Dispute not with the People of the Book (Jewish and Christian Bible)
> save in the fairer manner, except for
> those of them that do wrong and say
> "We believe in what has been sent down
> to us, and what has been sent down to you;

Our God and your God is One and to Him we have surrendered." (Armstrong 1992, 160)

So Muhammad had found a way of rebutting the Jews without abandoning his central belief that people must surrender to God, not to the mundane rules and regulations of the particular faith.

Later in his public life, Muhammad applied political frame principles to his military encounters. He was well known for the humanitarian way in which he dealt with prisoners and liberally engaged in prisoner exchanges. These practices were a reflection of Muhammad's thinking. He was ready to die for his faith, but he was also ready to compromise on what he considered to be the nonessentials. He even offered to marry the daughter of the leader of an enemy tribe if she converted to Islam. In marrying Aisha, he transformed the enemy tribe into an ally.

To Muhammad, the purpose of any war must be to restore peace and harmony as soon as possible. Much as some may be repulsed by the spectacle of his many battles, it can be argued that politically it was the right thing to do to allow all parties to live in peace. In winning the Battle of the Trench, he had defeated the powerful Jewish tribes and shown that he would tolerate no further treachery against the Muslims. He had become the most powerful man in Arabia and had brought to a speedy end a bloody conflict that, had he not used an abundant amount of political frame leadership behavior in the Treaty of Hudaybiyyah, could have dragged on for years. "Whatever condition Quraysh (the Jewish tribes) made in which they ask me to show kindness to kindred, I will agree to," he said (Armstrong 1992, 216).

Lastly, Muhammad was keenly aware that some Muslim converts, especially those in conquered lands, remained true to their former religion. But he made no effort to enforce strict theological orthodoxy, instead hoping that his employment of political frame leadership behavior would eventually lead to their religious surrender to Islam. Thus, he almost single-handedly managed to accomplish what became known as Pax Islamica.

THE MORAL FRAME

As mentioned earlier, the moral frame is my own contribution to situational leadership theory. In my view, the moral frame completes situational leadership theory. Without it, leaders could just as easily use their leadership skills for promoting evil as for promoting good. Leaders operating out of the moral frame are concerned about their obligations and responsibilities to their followers. Moral frame leaders use some type of moral compass to direct their behavior. They practice what has been described as servant leadership and are concerned with those individuals and groups that are marginalized in their organizations and in society. In short, they are concerned about social justice.

There is no question that Muhammad developed a moral lens through which he filtered his leadership behavior. He codified that lens in the form of a book that became known as the Quran (Word of God). As we have seen, the five pillars of Islam, one of which is a concern for the needy, were developed from the Quran and serve as the moral compass of all Muslims. And Khadija, one of Muhammad's early mentors, gave testimony to Muhammad's use of the moral frame when she said: "You are kind and considerate toward your kin. You help the poor and the forlorn and bear their burdens. You are striving to restore the high moral qualities that our people have lost (Armstrong 1992, 85).

KEY IDEAS

There is much evidence that Muhammad practiced a form of situational leadership. As we have seen, he was active in all five frames under appropriate conditions. One might argue that he spent an inordinate amount of time in one or another of the frames, or that he went to the extreme in one or another frame, but it is difficult to deny the results.

The Islamic religion that he created has over a billion members worldwide and is the fastest-growing major religion on the globe. There is much for leaders and aspiring leaders to learn from observing and analyzing the leadership behavior of one of the most influential and charismatic men in recorded history.

Chapter Eight

Mahatma Gandhi

The weak can never forgive. Forgiveness is the attribute of the strong.
—Mahatma Gandhi

Mahatma Gandhi was born in India in 1869 and is most remembered for his dedication to nonviolent resistance and its use in gaining India's independence from Great Britain. Many civil rights and religious leaders, including Martin Luther King Jr. and St. Mother Teresa, used Gandhi's concept of nonviolent protest, which he called *satyagraha*, as a model for their leadership behavior.

In 1888, Gandhi left India to study law in London. He successfully passed the bar in 1891. Gandhi unsuccessfully attempted to practice law in India, so after a couple of years took a position in Natal, South Africa.

While traveling by train from Natal to the South African capital, railroad officials told Gandhi that he would be required to transfer to the third-class passenger car even though he held a first-class ticket. Gandhi refused to move and a policeman came and escorted him from the train. As a result of this and other similar experiences, Gandhi spent the next twenty years working for the advancement of Indians' rights in South Africa.

Finally, in 1915, Gandhi returned to India. He almost immediately entered the struggle for independence from England. He employed nonviolent civil disobedience as his primary strategy in the struggle against British suppression. Gandhi took advantage of the Amritsar Massacre of civilians by British troops to further the drive for independence.

In 1930, Gandhi launched a new nonviolent campaign against the tax on salt that the British had recently imposed. This campaign was highlighted by Gandhi's famous march to the sea where he made salt himself. Thousands of Indians followed him on the march to the seacoast town of Dandi.

Gandhi intensified his demands for independence, authoring a resolution called "Quit India." Although he was instrumental in the ultimate decision by England to grant India its independence, he never lived to see it. On January 30, 1948, Gandhi was shot and killed during his nightly public walk on the grounds of his community when a radical Hindu assassin took his life because he felt that Gandhi's compassion for the Muslims weakened the Hindus (Marcello 2006; Pastan 2006).

SITUATIONAL LEADERSHIP ANALYSIS

Situational models of leadership differ from earlier trait and behavioral models in asserting that no single way of leading works in all situations. Rather, appropriate behavior depends on the circumstances at a given time. Effective managers diagnose the situation, identify the leadership style or behavior that will be most effective, and then determine whether they can implement the required style.

Although he is primarily known as a human resource and symbolic leader, Mahatma Gandhi was adept at utilizing all four leadership frames suggested by Bolman and Deal (1991). Furthermore, he ran virtually all of his leadership behavior through a self-imposed moral lens. Early in his professional career, while living in South Africa, he stressed the need to be situational with his growing cadre of followers. He implored them to come together as a group, despite their varied faiths—Hindu, Parsi, Muslim, and Christian—and urged them to abandon their comfort zone and learn English so that they could better represent themselves in South African society.

Gandhi modeled the situational nature of leadership for his disciples. Among Europeans living in South Africa, Indians were seen as unclean, although the urban Indians, such as Gandhi and other professionals living in Natal, saw themselves as highly civilized. Still, Gandhi was known as a "coolie barrister" in South Africa, and he knew that continuing to wear his turban would only reinforce the stereotype. If he was forced to remove his turban, he would be swallowing an insult. This was not something Gandhi could endure, so he changed his turban to a Western-style hat and avoided any confrontations. Later in life, after he had established his reputation, he dressed the way he wanted.

When one method did not work, Gandhi was disappointed but never disheartened. He merely pursued other ways to strengthen and unite the South African Indian community. For example, he founded a weekly journal called the *Indian Opinion*, which featured educational and informational articles on such varied topics as politics, diet, health, and sanitary habits.

Having initially tried and failed with the traditional methods of opposing laws, such as lobbying against them and threatening to vote legislators out of office, Gandhi looked for an opportunity to apply an alternative approach—*satyagraha*, or civil disobedience—to the situation. The opportunity came in 1907 after the government of Transvaal, South Africa, passed a law that became known as the Black Act. It required Indians living in Transvaal to be fingerprinted and to carry registration cards. Special taxes were also imposed, and Hindu marriages were not recognized by the state. Gandhi was outraged at this egregious act of discrimination. Thus he advised the Indian community to disobey the law.

When civil disobedience began to lose its impact, Gandhi moved to a different method of opposing oppression. With unemployment and salaries among the Indian population in South Africa growing even worse than before, Gandhi sensed that his strategy of civil disobedience was not working and placing too much hardship on poor laborers. He decided to strengthen their determination by going on strike himself—a hunger strike. He pledged to fast, or refrain from eating, until the workers' demands were met. With the press covering his actions and the country concerned that he would become a martyr, the mill owners capitulated.

Being the situational leader that he was, he was always looking for new and different ways of achieving his goals, but always within the parameters of nonviolence. He called for government officials to stop working in the service of the Crown and for lawyers to abandon the courts. He urged students to boycott government schools and for soldiers to desert their posts. He persuaded ordinary citizens not to pay government taxes. Through his newspaper *Young India* and frequent speeches, his ideas began to draw support.

Gandhi retained the flexibility of a situational leader throughout his life. For example, even though Gandhi did not condone the violence and inhumanity of war, he wanted to help the Allies in some way, so he established an ambulance corps to transport injured men from the battlefield during World War I. He was not daunted by British officials who were prejudiced and believed that Indians were cowardly and would not take the risk of going into a war zone. Gandhi went forward anyway, and the ambulance corps proved effective (Marcello 2006; Pastan 2006).

THE STRUCTURAL FRAME

Structural leaders develop a new model of the relationship of structure, strategy, and environment for their organizations. Strategic planning, extensive preparation, and effecting change are priorities for them. Although he was not primarily known as a structural leader, we shall see that, being the situational leader that he was, Gandhi depended on structural frame leadership behavior when it was appropriate to do so.

As a young man, Gandhi no sooner arrived in South Africa than he began utilizing structural leadership behavior. The government was about to pass a law depriving Indians of their right to elect members of the Natal Legislative Assembly. In effect, they would have no representation in local government. Gandhi thought the bill was extremely dangerous. "It is the first nail into our coffin," he said. "It strikes at the root of our self respect" (Pastan 2006, 45). Gandhi immediately canceled his passage back to India. He would stay in South Africa and fight the franchise bill by obtaining more than ten thousand signatures in a petition against the bill.

When the franchise bill passed, Gandhi was not daunted and in true structural frame form planned to follow through with sustained agitation. He wanted Lord Ripon, the colonial secretary in London, to veto the bill and saw constant pressure as the only means of attaining his cooperation. To achieve this goal, he and his Indian friends decided to create a viable political organization to run their campaigns, the Natal Indian Congress. As few members were accustomed to public speaking, Gandhi taught them the rules of parliamentary procedure and the fine points of public speaking. He used this type of structural leadership behavior for the remainder of his life.

Gandhi continued his focus on structural frame leadership behavior for the next three years as he organized a thriving legal practice and established the Natal Indian Congress, which organized opposition to injustice and discrimination. Its publications were widely circulated, even in Britain, where many of the queen's subjects could learn of their fellow citizens in another part of the empire who were often governed by unjust laws fueled by prejudice.

In addition to opposing British oppression, Gandhi used structural frame leadership enactments to correct some of the prejudices among his own people. In view of his goal of someday breaking the caste taboos, and emphasizing that all honest work was worthy, Gandhi volunteered for clerical duty at the National Congress and was given the task of answering correspondence. This meekness paid off, as it helped him to know the men and to understand the workings of the Congress. In only a few days, Gandhi would be ready to use his position as an instrument for action.

Eventually, Gandhi's leadership behavior produced results. At a mass meeting in Johannesburg, three thousand Indians led by Gandhi resolved to fight the Black Act. Together, he and his followers set goals and made plans to protest what they believed was an unjust law. It was in protestation of this law that the idea of *satyagraha*, or peaceful civil disobedience, took root.

By the time he returned to India, Gandhi had honed his use of structural frame leadership behavior in the form of very effective peaceful protest and civil disobedience. In response to yet another British tax, this time on imported cotton, Gandhi reacted in true structural leadership form. India had its own cotton-spinning and cotton-weaving traditions. If people relearned how to spin cotton into thread, Gandhi reasoned, they would not have to import it, and the art of spinning and weaving in India would be revived, and under his leadership the Indian spinning and weaving industry was indeed revived.

Continuing his structural leadership behavior in protest of the salt tax, whereby Indians were mandated to buy heavily taxed salt from England, Gandhi wrote a letter to Lord Irwin, viceroy of India, proclaiming that the tax was evil. He declared: "If my letter makes no appeal to your heart, on the eleventh day of this month, I shall proceed with such co-workers of the Ashram as I can take, to disregard the provisions of the Salt Laws" (Pastan 2006, 81). Receiving no response, Gandhi then organized his legendary Dandi salt march, in which he and thousands of his followers marched 248 miles to the sea and made salt themselves. Over sixty thousand of Gandhi's disciples were imprisoned as a result of the march.

Later, after World War II, when the Quit India movement went into full force, Gandhi utilized structural frame leadership behavior in planning and organizing marches and protests down to the last detail. He also developed well-thought-out strategies, like hunger strikes, and applied them at just the right time to maximize their effectiveness. As we have seen, although Gandhi is best known for his use of the human resource, symbolic, and even the political frames, he also used the structural frame of leadership to great effect (Marcello 2006; Pastan 2006).

THE HUMAN RESOURCE FRAME

Human resource leaders believe in people and communicate that belief. They are passionate about productivity through people. This frame is one of Mahatma Gandhi's strongest. He had great respect and empathy for humankind.

Gandhi placed great value on human dignity and devoted his life to the pursuit of human rights for everyone. Virtually all of his efforts were devoted to obtaining justice for all individuals, no matter their status in society. In South Africa, he organized peasants, farmers, and urban laborers in protesting excessive land taxation and discrimination, and he did so in a nonviolent way. He led thousands in the Dandi salt march, protesting the unjust and discriminatory British salt tax.

Later, in India, he organized and led the Quit India campaign that ultimately gained Indian independence from Great Britain. Even though he was a devout Hindu, he was very ecumenical in dealing with people of other faiths. He was very much against the partition of India into India and Pakistan because he believed that, given time, the Hindus and Muslims would learn to live peaceably alongside one another. Suffice it to say, the human resource frame was at the foundation of Gandhi's leadership behavior.

Chapter 8
THE SYMBOLIC FRAME

In the symbolic frame, the organization is seen as a stage, a theater in which every actor plays certain roles, and the symbolic leader attempts to communicate the right impressions to the right audiences.

Gandhi began his use of symbolic frame enactments at a very young age and to establish himself as a man of integrity. Even as a schoolboy, he feared telling a lie. When he misspelled the word *kettle* during the education inspector's visit to his high school, his teacher secretly prodded him with the point of his boot, hoping to prompt Gandhi to copy the correct spelling from his neighbor's slate. But Gandhi could not understand why the teacher was kicking him. It would never have occurred to him to use the work of another student. So while the rest of the class sailed through the exercise, Gandhi stumbled. Later in his life, this same love for the truth and his stubborn attachment to it would spur him to lead millions of Indians in the fight for independence from British rule.

As a young lawyer in South Africa, Gandhi used symbolic frame leadership behavior to make many of his points. For example, Gandhi was already feeling the disapproval of the white classes when he entered the courts, but when the magistrate asked him to remove his turban, he became particularly angry. Unwilling to yield to the magistrate's request, Gandhi walked out. Afterward, he wrote to the local newspaper defending the wearing of turbans in court on cultural grounds. The press criticized the "unwelcome visitor," but some people supported him, and the turban remained part of Gandhi's attire, at least for the time being (Pastan 2006, 39).

On another occasion, Gandhi was asked to move to a third-class seat, despite having a first-class ticket. Like Rosa Parks did after him, Gandhi refused to be denied. Finally, he was physically thrown from the train, but in doing so, he had made his point and embellished his growing reputation.

In the process of peaceably protesting yet another unjust and discriminatory British tax in South Africa, Gandhi was met by an angry mob armed with bricks. A quick-thinking police superintendent's wife protected him from the crowd and saved him from being badly beaten. However, Gandhi would not press charges. He did not want his attackers punished. He wanted the system responsible for their actions changed, and he continued his fight for Indians in the courts and in the press.

Gandhi wanted to set an example for other Indians in South Africa, so even though he was wealthy enough to have servants, he learned to wash and iron his own clothes and even cut his own hair. When his third child, Ramdas, was born, Gandhi assisted in the delivery. He expected the whole family to share in all household tasks, even emptying the chamber pots. Later, he and his followers lived in self-sufficient settlements. There, living first in tents with no comforts or conveniences and then in houses made of corrugated metal, Gandhi and his disciples worked, farmed, and ran the printing press.

Gandhi wrote two pamphlets for the purpose of propagandizing. In the first, *An Appeal to Every Briton in South Africa*, he wrote in regard to the Indian franchise law, which imposed stringent and discriminatory voter-registration regulations on Indians. "To say that the Indian does not understand the franchise is to ignore the whole history of India. Representation in the truest sense of the term, the Indian has understood and appreciated from the earliest ages. That principle—the Panchayat—guides all the actions of the Indian. He considers himself a member of the Panchayat, which really is the whole body civic to which he belongs for the time being" (Marcello 2006, 49). The second work, entitled *The Indian Franchise: An Appeal*, also pleaded for support in blocking the franchise measure.

As mentioned earlier, Gandhi engaged in symbolic frame leadership behavior when, during the Boer War between the Zulus and the British, he volunteered to become involved. He had no hostile feelings toward the Zulus, but as a British subject, he thought it disloyal to the empire to support them. Having been refused membership in the British army, Gandhi, in a symbolic gesture, organized an ambulance corps.

The Zulu rebellion made Gandhi ponder even more the principles guiding his life—truth, nonviolence, self-realization, and community service. Understanding that a commitment to these goals meant acquiring greater spiritual strength, he decided to take a vow of *brahmacharya*—control of the senses and the abstinence from material goods and physical pleasures. By disciplining oneself in this way he believed that one's inner strength could be developed to the point where one would have the fortitude to practice nonviolence and civil disobedience despite the serious risks of beatings, imprisonment, and possibly death.

As a result of his various protests, Gandhi spent much of his life in prison, sometimes doing hard labor. But he never complained. Rather, he passed his days reading and praying. He believed that the real path to happiness lay in suffering for the interests of one's country, humanity, and religion, and he consciously went about molding these desirable behaviors.

Hailed by native Indians for his success in South Africa, he was warmly welcomed home in 1916. They called him *Mahatma*, which means "Great Soul." Upon returning to India, Gandhi went directly to see Gopal Gokhaele, his political mentor. Knowing that Gandhi was eager to practice civil disobedience in India, Gokhaele cautioned him to take time to reconnect with the country. Gandhi hoped to establish a settlement house in India but instead took Gokhaele's advice and spent a year touring the country first.

He began cultivating his future image by symbolically wearing clothes more typical of a laborer than a lawyer: a loincloth from an Indian mill and a cap. Using only third-class transportation, the young man who had been physically removed from his first-class compartment in South Africa now chose to share the discomfort and inconvenience of common passengers. He witnessed the officials' contempt for his fellow travelers and realized just how much work he would have to do to change a system that allowed human beings to be treated in such a discriminatory and inhumane way.

Gandhi was further disillusioned by the so-called Massacre of Amritsar, when a peaceful protest of British rule was met by violence. In an effort to escape the bullets, some of the protesters dove into a well and drowned. Twenty minutes of firing left 379 dead and 1,200 wounded. Afterward, General Dyer, the leader of the nearby military compound, would not let any Indians into the compound to help the wounded. He later said cavalierly, "It was not my job. Hospitals were open and they could have gone there" (Pastan 2006, 67).

The great Indian poet Rabindranath Tagore exhibited some symbolic frame leadership behavior of his own and renounced his knighthood, stating in a letter of protest, "The time has come when the badges of honor make our shame glaring in their incongruous context of humiliation, and I for my part wish to stand shorn of all special distinctions, by the side of those of my countrymen who, for their so-called insignificance, are liable to suffer degradation not fit for human beings" (Pastan 2006, 68).

Gandhi took his cue from Tagore and engaged in some symbolic frame leadership behavior himself by returning the medals he had earned for his service in the Boer War and the Zulu rebellion, and he asked Indians of all religions to join him in a long, hard struggle for *swaragi*, or self-rule. Gandhi began educating people about *satyagraha* through two newspapers, *Young India* in English and *Navajivan* in Gujarati, and he became involved in the Indian National Congress. In 1920, he became the president of the All India Home Rule League.

A formal campaign against the British began to take shape. There was to be a policy of noncooperation in cities, towns, and villages throughout the subcontinent. Dressed only in his trademark handwoven dhoti, shawl, and sandals, Gandhi traveled throughout the provinces, spreading his message. Over time, Gandhi would become even more of a hero to the Indians and a serious threat to British rule.

Yet, just as the movement reached its apex, it ended abruptly after a violent clash in the town of Chauri Chaura in 1922. Fearing that the movement was about to take a turn toward violence and convinced that this would be the undoing of all his work, Gandhi called off the campaign of mass civil disobedience. Gandhi was arrested, and in a typically symbolic act, he pleaded guilty on all counts and told the court, "I should have known the consequences of every one of my acts. I know them. I knew that I was playing with fire. I ran the risk, and if I was set free, I would still do the same" (Pastan 2006, 75).

While Gandhi was in prison, the Indian National Congress and the cooperation among Hindus and Muslims began to break down. In another instance of symbolic leadership behavior, Gandhi engaged in his first great fast in order to teach the lesson of tolerance, even if it literally killed him. His fast had the intended result. On the twenty-first day, a unity conference was organized to discuss a peaceful resolution.

Under Gandhi's guidance, the Indian National Congress issued a declaration of independence from England on January 26, 1930. Unlike the American Declaration of Independence, Gandhi intended to wage war against the empire with *satyagraha* instead of swords and guns. One of his first efforts at civil disobedience was the protestation of the salt tax with the Great Salt March to the sea. When he arrived, Gandhi bathed in the sea as a symbol of purification. On his way back to the beach, he bent down and picked up some salt that had been brought in by the tide. With this simple act, he had broken the law.

However, at the outset of the 1930 Congress, with dominion status still not granted to India and without any progress toward that end, delegates and the new president of the Congress, Jawaharlal Nehru, under Gandhi's direction, prepared another series of *satyagrahas*, fully intending to win autonomy. The battle cry would be *Purna Swaraj!*, meaning "complete independence." The entire nation took a pledge to win independence or die trying. In a draft of the people's pledge, Gandhi stated that India had been ruined economically, politically, culturally, and spiritually, and he wrote, "We hold it to be a crime against men and God to submit any longer to a rule that has caused this fourfold disaster to our country" (Marcello 2006, 140).

A few days later, Gandhi also published a list of reforms that were required if England was to avoid national civil disobedience. Included in the list were a reduction in military expenditures by 50 percent, a levy of a protective tariff on foreign cloth, the discharge of all political prisoners, and the abolition of the salt tax.

Upon the outbreak of World War II, Gandhi once again utilized symbolic frame leadership behavior. He firmly believed that violence never solved anything and wrote to Adolf Hitler, "It is quite clear that you are today the one person in the world who can prevent a war which may reduce humanity to the savage state" (Pastan 2006, 91).

Gandhi was further distraught by Hitler's persecution of the Jews. He wrote, "If there ever could be a justifiable war in the name of and for humanity, war against Germany would be completely justified." But Gandhi continued to insist, despite Hitler's evil government, "I do not believe in any war" (Pastan 2006, 92). Some of his ideas were deeply troubling to those most threatened by Hitler's tyranny. He suggested, for example, that Jews practice *satyagraha* and that the British let Hitler take their island rather than fight.

After a lifetime of seeking peace, Gandhi was assassinated by a Hindu extremist in 1948, when he was seventy-eight years old. The effectiveness of his leadership behavior, specifically his symbolic behavior, can be judged by the words of Jawaharlal Nehru, the prime minister of India, upon Gandhi's death.

> The light has gone out of our lives and there is darkness everywhere and I do not quite know what to tell you and how to say it. Our beloved leader, Bapu as we call him, the father of our nation, is no more. The light has gone out, I said, and yet I was wrong. For the light that shone in this country was no ordinary light. The light that has illumined this country for so many years will illumine this country for many more years, and the world will see it and it will give solace to innumerable hearts. For that light represented the living truth, and the eternal man was with us with his eternal truth reminding us of the right path, drawing us from error, and taking this ancient country to freedom. (Pastan 2006, 112)

Gandhi believed that if one freed oneself from rage, one could accomplish good for all mankind. In effect, he took Jesus's message, "love your enemy," to a whole new level. In one last example of his symbolic frame leadership behavior, Gandhi left the world the following message of hope: "We may never be strong enough to be entirely nonviolent, in thought, word, and deed. But we must keep nonviolence as our goal and make steady progress towards it. The truth of a few will count. The untruth of millions will vanish even like chaff before a whiff of wind" (Pastan 2006, 120).

THE POLITICAL FRAME

Leaders operating out of the political frame clarify what they want and what they can get. Political leaders are realists above all. They never let what they want cloud their judgment about what is possible. They assess the distribution of power and interests. They are all about "making friends and influencing people."

Mahatma Gandhi made frequent use of political frame leadership behavior. For example, when he first came to South Africa, Gandhi's friends had become more militant regarding the Indian agenda, and some thought Gandhi had betrayed them by removing his head covering. Gandhi reasoned with them, saying it was the custom that no hats of any kind were to be worn in the Supreme Court and that he had only complied with those customs. He had come to truly appreciate the pragmatism of compromise, a policy that would come to play a significant role in his philosophy of nonviolence in later years.

In 1914, after much protestation, Gandhi and General Jan Christiaan Smuts reached a political agreement that all Hindu and Muslim marriages in

South Africa would be recognized, and Indians would no longer be subject to unfair taxes. Even though the immigration law would remain in effect, Gandhi was pleased with the gains that *satyagraha* had won for his countrymen. In both a political and symbolic frame gesture, he sent General Smuts a pair of sandals he had made while in prison.

Gandhi often used political leadership behavior in assessing the readiness level of his followers for engaging effectively in nonviolent civil disobedience. In one instance, he was arrested in South Africa and deported to Bombay. There he heard about violent acts occurring in the name of *satyagraha* in other Indian cities and realized that tensions were too great and the people too unschooled in nonviolence to make strikes and other protests successful. Thus he called off the protests.

The Amritsar Massacre turned Gandhi from a social activist into a political one as well. In 1921, he became the head of the Indian National Congress. The Congress had previously been open only to Indian intellectuals. It served as a forum for those who wished to air their views about British rule and was mainly loyal to the empire. Gandhi drafted a new constitution for the Congress. Under his direction, the Congress began to have an independent voice and reached out to all classes of Indians, both educated and uneducated.

In 1931, in the midst of his nonviolent protests over British rule in India, when over sixty thousand protesters had been jailed, Gandhi and the viceroy reached a political agreement that they both hoped would calm the waters, and Gandhi did not want to jeopardize the gains made by the salt march. The compromise agreement included the following:

- Discontinuance of the civil disobedience movement.
- Congress' agreement to participate in the Round Table Conference.
- Withdrawal of all governmental regulations meant to impede Congress.
- Withdrawal of all convictions that did not pertain to violent actions.
- Release of all prisoners who had participated in the civil disobedience movement.

Members of both sides were disenchanted, each believing that their side had given too much. But Gandhi convinced his followers that this was the best compromise that could be reached under current conditions.

Gandhi used political frame leadership behavior to extract concessions from England in exchange for India's all-out participation in World War II. India would have dominion status, similar to Canada's arrangement, when the war ended. In addition, India's provinces, princely states, and minorities could, if they desired, have separate settlement agreements with the British. Also, after the war, these individual territories could withdraw from the British Commonwealth if they wished.

However, the British insisted that India be divided into many parts to assimilate the various ethnic groups. This provision turned out to be the deal breaker when Gandhi could not in good conscience accept a fragmented India. So he officially opposed the war and would not approve of India's involvement in it. Nevertheless, Gandhi's persistence proved successful when, after the war, Great Britain finally granted independence to India.

When, in the advent of India's independence, Indian Muslims threatened to destroy India if they could not have a separate Pakistan, Gandhi once again used political frame leadership behavior. With no other recourse, Lord Mountbatten, with Gandhi's support, finally capitulated. In typical political frame thinking, Gandhi reasoned that independence for two countries was better than no independence at all. India would be free but divided.

On August 15, 1947, the ancient land of the Mongols was divided into two nations: India and Pakistan. Gandhi had long anticipated the moment when the two-hundred-year reign of Britain would end. But when he was asked to be the president of India, once again he engaged in political frame leadership behavior by authoring an article in *Young India* convincing his constituents that he was not the logical choice for president because of his age and potential health problems. He encouraged his young disciple Nehru's election. Gandhi knew that with Nehru in office he would be able to lead with or without the title.

THE MORAL FRAME

The moral frame is my own contribution to situational leadership theory. In my view, the moral frame completes situational leadership theory. Without it, leaders could just as easily use their leadership skills for promoting evil as for promoting good. Leaders operating out of the moral frame are concerned about their obligations and responsibilities to their followers. Moral frame leaders use some type of moral compass to direct their behavior. They practice what has been described as servant leadership or leading with heart and are concerned with those individuals and groups that are marginalized in their organizations and in society. In short, they are concerned about equality, fairness, and social justice.

There is little question that Mahatma Gandhi was a great believer in the necessity of operating out of the moral frame. One could argue that his every action was examined through a moral lens. He developed such a moral lens through his concept of *satyagraha*—nonviolent protest. In his native language, *satya* means "truth," and *agraha* means "firmness." Using this as his guide, he engaged in a nonviolent moral war against persecution and injustice.

In chapter 2, it was suggested that in order to make leadership a moral science, one should consider using the Ignatian Vision as a guide to one's leadership practice. The Ignatian Vision posits a concern for the *magis* (the more), discernment, *cura personalis* (care of the person), service to others, and social justice. Mahatma Gandhi's leadership behavior showed evidence that he shared Ignatius's concern for these ideals. He sought perfection (the *magis*) in the form of truth in all of his thoughts and actions; he engaged in discernment in determining the best course of action for attaining his social justice agenda; he had great respect for human dignity; he devoted his life to service of others; and he was sensitive to those like the untouchables and others who were on the margins of society. In short, like every other leader profiled here, Mahatma Gandhi was a model of the effective use of moral frame leadership behavior.

KEY IDEAS

Gandhi's work to lift the untouchables of India from a life of squalor and shame bore fruit in India and served as an inspiration to oppressed classes throughout the world, from African Americans in America's segregated South to black South Africans living under apartheid. His appeal to people of all races and religions to lead a moral, truthful life spread far beyond India.

For Gandhi, the world's poor had a very human face. He asked his fellow man to "recall the face of the poorest and most helpless man you have ever seen and ask yourself if the step you contemplate is going to be of any use to him" (Pastan 2006, 112). These words were almost exactly echoed fifty years later by St. Mother Teresa in her work with the world's poor.

In many ways, Mahatma Gandhi could be considered the prototype for the effective use of situational leadership behavior. He appropriately balanced his leadership behavior both across and within the five leadership frames. St. Mother Teresa of Calcutta and Martin Luther King Jr. are just two of many leaders throughout the world who have effectively modeled their leadership behavior after that of Mahatma Gandhi.

Chapter Nine

Martin Luther King Jr.

To succeed we need to get the PhD's, the MD's and NoD's together in a common cause.

—*Martin Luther King Jr.*

Martin Luther King Jr. was born on January 15, 1929, in Atlanta, Georgia. He was a prominent leader in the American civil rights movement in the 1950s and 1960s. In 1955, he led the Montgomery Bus Boycott and helped found the Southern Christian Leadership Conference, serving as its first president. His efforts led to the 1963 March on Washington, where King delivered his famous "I Have a Dream" speech. There, he raised public consciousness to the civil rights movement and established himself as one of the greatest orators in US history.

In 1964, King became the youngest person to receive the Nobel Peace Prize for his work to end segregation and racial discrimination through civil disobedience and other nonviolent means. By the time of his death in 1968, he had refocused his efforts on ending poverty and opposing the Vietnam War, both from a moral perspective.

King was assassinated on April 4, 1968, in Memphis, Tennessee. He was posthumously awarded the Presidential Medal of Freedom in 1977 and Congressional Gold Medal in 2004; Martin Luther King Jr. Day was established as a national holiday in the United States in 1986.

Always a brilliant student, he entered Morehouse College at the age of fifteen.

On March 29, 1968, King went to Memphis, Tennessee in support of the black sanitary public works employees. On April 3, King addressed a rally and delivered his "I've been to the Mountaintop" address in which he predicted his death. As fate would have it, his prediction came true and he was shot to death a day after the speech. Two months after his death, escaped convict James Earl Ray was captured at London's Heathrow Airport and confessed to the assassination (Oates 1982).

SITUATIONAL LEADERSHIP ANALYSIS

Situational models of leadership differ from earlier trait and behavioral models in asserting that no single way of leading works in all situations. Rather, appropriate behavior depends on the circumstances at a given time. Effective managers diagnose the situation, identify the leadership style or behavior that will be most effective, and then determine whether they can implement the required style. Martin Luther King Jr. was an astute practitioner of situational leadership theory. As we shall see, he realized the need to adapt his leadership style to the situation and was very adept at doing so.

Dr. King recognized the need to be situational in applying his leadership behavior and described himself as an "ambivert," which he defined as a cross between an extravert and an introvert. He liked to quote a French philosopher who once said: "No man is strong unless he bears within this character antitheses strongly marked" (Oates 1982, 41). King also pointed out that Jesus too had recognized the need for blending opposites when he commanded us to be both tough-minded and tender hearted. And although King could be tough-minded as an intellectual, he was tender hearted in his treatment of people.

When King first began his ministry, his sermons tended to be somber and intellectual, like a classroom lecture. But he soon came to understand the emotional role of the Negro church, to realize how much black folks needed this precious sanctuary to vent their frustrations and let themselves go. So he let himself go. The first "Amen!" from his congregation would set him off to illustrating his intellectual points with dazzling oratory. For what was good preaching if not "a mixture of emotion and intellect?" he declared (Oates 1982, 56). As we shall see, King did not restrict himself to one or two of the five leadership frames. Rather, in true situational leadership fashion, he utilized all five when appropriate.

THE STRUCTURAL FRAME

Structural frame leaders seek to develop a new model of the relationship of structure, strategy, and environment for their organizations. Strategic planning, extensive preparation, and effecting change are priorities for them. Martin Luther King Jr. was very active in this frame of leadership. His ideologies were well thought out and internalized, and he planned strategically to achieve the goals that he derived from them.

Most black preachers urged their congregations to expect their reward in heaven, but King, acting out of the structural frame, shuddered at such a negative approach to race relations. Yet W. E. B. DuBois and Marcus Garvey did not have the solution, either. How indeed were African Americans to combat discrimination in a country ruled by a white majority?

A class assignment in Thoreau's "Civil Disobedience" offered a clue, introducing King to the idea of passive resistance. King was probably aware of the blacks' civil disobedience then taking place in America. As early as 1947, A. Philip Randolph threatened to lead a protest march if the armed services were not desegregated (President Truman subsequently did desegregate them), and the Congress of Racial Equality (CORE) conducted little-publicized "stand ins" and "freedom rides." King, however, was infatuated with Thoreau's argument that a creative minority could set in motion a moral revolution—and that is what he set about doing.

With 70 percent of its riders gone during the Montgomery bus boycott, the police commissioner ordered Negro taxi companies to charge the legal minimum rate per customer, thus ending cheap taxi fares for boycotters. In another instance of King's use of structural frame leadership behavior, King moved quickly to meet this crisis. He countered by devising an ingenious car pool. Volunteer Negro drivers transported people to and from work, operating out of forty-eight dispatch and forty-two pickup stations established in key sections of the city. The car pool was so efficient that a local white judge later praised it as the best transportation system Montgomery ever had.

King founded the Southern Christian Leadership Conference (SCLC) as a vehicle that would operate through the Southern Negro Church and function as a service agency to coordinate local civil rights activity—exactly what a structural leader would do. The SCLC's main goal was to bring the Negro masses into the freedom struggle by expanding "the Montgomery way" across the South.

In this way it differed significantly from the National Association for the Advancement of Colored People (NAACP) (mostly legal), the National Urban League (focus on northern cities), or CORE (also, mostly in the North, but according to some, not too effective). The SCLC's initial project was a southern-wide voter registration drive called the "Crusade for Citizenship" to commence on Lincoln's birthday—a symbolic frame leadership gesture. Again demonstrating structural frame leadership behavior after the Montgomery bus boycott, King went on to outline what the Negro must struggle for in the coming new age. "We must seek the ballot," he said, "so that we will no longer be the convenient tool of unscrupulous politicians" (Oates 1982, 123).

And so the Crusade for Citizenship was on, with the SCLC exhorting affiliate churches to run voting clinics and canvass black neighborhoods urging all eligible Negroes to turn out for voter registration. In another display of structural frame leadership enactment, King prepared for a full-scale assault on all forms of segregation, by establishing an SCLC training program that would instruct youths and adult leaders in nonviolence and then send them into their communities to launch mass-action programs against segregated schools and eating and transportation facilities. So that he could devote full-time to the SCLC, King resigned his position at Dexter Avenue Baptist Church in Montgomery and moved to Atlanta, where he worked only part-time at his father's church.

In the rare instances where his strategies did not work, like the failed Albany Movement, a Georgia civil rights protest, King used structural frame behavior to conduct a postmortem analysis to determine where he and his followers went wrong. King and his staff conceded that they should not have obeyed the federal court injunction and that it had "broken our backs." King's inability to stay in jail had also hurt the movement, and so had Chief Pritchett's clever tactics. "We were naïve enough to think we could fill up the jails" (Pritchett bused the prisoners to adjoining towns' jails). Worse still, the SCLC had charged into Albany without proper planning and preparation. "We didn't know then how to mobilize people in masses and our protest was so vague," King concluded (Oates 1982, 199).

But in true structural frame mode, King learned from his mistakes. He and his followers had no intention of dashing blindly into Birmingham as they had in Albany. At a three-day retreat, held at the SCLC's training center in Dorchester, Georgia, King and his aides and advisors worked out a detailed plan called Project C, for Confrontation Birmingham. They would escalate the marches, tighten up the boycotts, even fill up the jails until they brought about a moment of "creative tension," when the evils of segregation would stand revealed and white merchants would be driven to the negotiating table.

By Christmas 1964, King and his staff had completed final plans for Project Alabama, the direct-action plan in Selma designed to win southern Negroes the unobstructed right to vote. In structural frame style, another organizing retreat was held. King intended to create a situation in Selma by applying all the skill and experience he had garnered in the battles at Albany, Birmingham, and St. Augustine. Selma had all the ingredients for King to make his point: a "nigger" section of town; the birthplace of the notorious segregationist police officer Bull Connor; and their spokesman was Sheriff Jim Clark, a burly, blusterous man who used crude language, a military swagger, and a tough-guy approach to civil rights.

After a number of successes in the South, King decided to move north with the campaign because he had worried for decades about the miseries of the ghetto blacks that the elective franchise alone could not alleviate. The question was, where to start? After much deliberation, he chose Chicago and developed a plan to convince the politicians to address the plight of the ghetto. "Egypt still exists in Chicago," he declared, "but the Pharaohs are more sophisticated and subtle" (Oates 1982, 380).

In yet another example of King's use of structural frame leadership behavior, he established the "poor-people's army" in Washington, D.C., to highlight the plight of Negroes in the slums. He and his staff completed a master plan for the Washington Campaign that involved recruiting blacks from all over to march on Washington and encamp in a plainly visible shantytown. He even thought of having a mule train traveling from Mississippi to Washington to dramatize the pilgrimage—combining symbolic frame behavior with structural frame behavior.

THE HUMAN RESOURCE FRAME

Human resource leaders believe in people and communicate that belief. They are passionate about *productivity through people*. Martin Luther King Jr. had a great capacity for practicing human resource leadership frame behavior. His entire life was dedicated to helping people, especially those marginalized in and by society.

King was very fond of Bayard Rustin, a bona fide intellectual who could talk with him about philosophical matters, and they enjoyed each other's company immensely. Rustin was once a member of the communist party and cautioned King about being too closely tied to him and what it could do to King's reputation. However, using human resource frame behavior, King said to him, "Look, we need everybody who can come to help us." Besides, Rustin's brush with communism had happened a long time before; he was certainly no communist when King knew him (Oates 1982, 94).

In another display of human resource frame enactment, when a deranged woman tried to kill him by stabbing him within a quarter inch of his heart, in typical human resource mode, King harbored no malice toward her. "Don't do anything to her," he counseled the authorities. "Don't prosecute her; get her healed," he said (Oates 1982, 140).

Ralph Abernathy, King's second in command, lacked intellectual strength and according to some had an insatiable need for recognition. But in King's eyes, Abernathy was a clever, adoring friend who was always there when King needed him. "I want you to know how much I appreciate your loyalty," he once told Abernathy. "I get all the attention from the press, but you're just as important to the movement as I am" (Oates 1982, 183).

In a true test of his devotion to human resource frame behavior, King even applied it to his enemies. Police Chief Laurie Pritchett, who was King's nemesis during the Albany Movement, placed King under round-the-clock police protection. As the campaign progressed, King developed a grudging respect for him. Once, King even canceled a demonstration so that Pritchett could spend the day with his wife. It was their wedding anniversary.

King's use of human resource behavior was recognized by his friends and colleagues. Andrew Young, one of his aides, said this of King:

> He had the strength, too, to be tender with people, listening patiently to their troubles, commiserating with them. In need of love himself, he could give love to others with enormous sensitivity.
>
> He was especially affectionate toward members of his executive staff, whom he treated like extended family that belonged to him. He was able to find that common bond of love and worth in each of us that would make us produce our best. We were strong-willed and it took a terrible amount of love to handle us. I would lose my temper, and Dr. King would caution me 'Hosea.' Just like that, where others would get angry with me around the table, he had the capacity to love me instead. (Oates 1982, 285)

THE SYMBOLIC FRAME

In the symbolic frame, the organization is seen as a stage, a theater in which every actor plays certain roles and the symbolic leader attempts to communicate the right impressions to the right audiences. Many consider the symbolic frame to be Martin Luther King Jr.'s strongest.

King's facility with the symbolic frame became evident at an early age. In the eleventh grade, he entered an oratorical contest sponsored by the Negro Elks in Georgetown. One of his favorite teachers accompanied him on what proved to be a memorable occasion. Speaking on "The Negro and the Constitution," King captured a prize with the force of his presentation.

That night, heading back to Atlanta on a crowded bus, he and his teacher reviewed the exciting events of the day. The bus stopped and some whites got on. There were no empty seats. The white driver came back and ordered King and the teacher to surrender their seats but King refused to budge. The driver threatened him, called him a black son-of-a-bitch, until at last he heeded his teacher's whispers and reluctantly got up. They stood in the aisle all the way home, jostled and thrown about as the bus sped down the highway. "That night will never leave my mind," King said later. "It was the angriest I have ever been in my life" (Oates 1982, 16).

In a similar incident, this time on a train, King was traveling back to Atlanta from New York. On this train trip the reality of segregation again reared its ugly head. As the train traveled through Virginia, King made his way to the dining car and started to sit down anywhere, as he had done on the way through New York and New Jersey.

But the train was in Dixie now, and the waiter led him to a rear table and pulled a curtain down to shield the white passengers from his presence. He sat there, staring at that curtain, unable to believe that others could find him offensive. "I felt," he said, "as though the curtain had dropped on my selfhood" (Oates 1982, 17).

During the Christmas holidays of 1949, King spent his time reading Karl Marx. He carefully scrutinized *Das Kapital*, the *Communist Manifesto*, and several interpretive studies of Marx and Lenin. He came away from this experience with Christian concern. Communism, he believed, was profoundly and fundamentally evil. The communists contemptuously dismissed God as a figure of man's imagination and religion as a product of fear, ignorance, and superstition.

According to the communist texts he read, class and economic conflict, not divine will, were the forces operating on man. Man did not need God. He could save himself and create a better world alone. As a result of these contradictions to Christian values, King engaged in symbolic frame leadership behavior and publicly dismissed communism as a viable ideology.

Second, King could not accept the communist tenet that "the ends justify the means." He could not agree with Lenin that to achieve a classless society, we must be ready to employ trickery, deceit, lawbreaking, and withholding and concealing truth. King also disdained communism's crippling totalitarianism, which he felt stripped man of his inalienable rights and shackled him to the state.

King worried further that communism may be in the world because Christianity had lost its way. In a sermon he enjoined the church to stop mouthing pious irrelevancies and sanctimonious trivialities and cease being what Voltaire termed "the opium of the people." Rather, it should concern itself anew with social justice—with the creation of a world unity in which all barriers of status, gender, and color are abolished.

At Crozer seminary in Chester, Pennsylvania, King graduated in 1951 with a BA degree in divinity at the top of his class. He displayed his penchant for symbolic frame behavior once again by giving the valedictory address, and won a $1,300 scholarship to the graduate school of his choice, which was Boston University's prestigious School of Theology, where he earned his PhD. As part of his dissertation, he made his life-guiding statement regarding humility: "Keep Martin Luther King in the background and God in the foreground and everything will be all right. Remember you're the channel of the gospel, not the source" (Oates 1982, 48).

King was prompted once again to engage in symbolic frame behavior in a Sunday service in Philadelphia. He had attended a lecture by Dr. Mordicai A. Johnson, president of Harvard. Dr. Johnson had just spent fifty days in India, and his lecture was on the life and teaching of Mahatma Gandhi. As King sat attentively in his seat, Johnson explained how Gandhi had forged "Soul Force"—the power of love or truth—into a vehicle for social change.

Johnson argued that the moral power of Gandhian nonviolence could improve race relations in America, too. This was a revelation to King, who had developed a hatred for whites. Now Gandhi showed him how to harness his anger and channel it into a positive and creative force.

So King took Thoreau's theory and gave it practical application in the form of nonviolent activities like strikes, boycotts, and protest marches, much as Gandhi had done. Furthermore, he espoused love of neighbor, but not in the commonly understood form of love, but as "agape"—the love in Christ's teachings that took one to any length to restore the all important community, and if necessary, to forgive seventy times seventy to preserve community.

Determined to practice what he preached, and engaging in both structural and symbolic frame leadership behavior, King launched an ambitious social-action program at Dexter. Under his supervision, committees formed to tend the sick and needy, help artists with promise, and administer scholarship funds for high school graduates. At the same time, a social and political action committee held forums on political developments and kept members apprised of NAACP activity in the South. It was through these activities that he first befriended Ralph Abernathy, pastor of the neighboring First Baptist Church.

Looking for an occasion to further his cause symbolically, King received great news in 1955 from his friends in the NAACP. They had come upon a perfect case. Rosa Parks, a tailor's assistant in a downtown Montgomery, Alabama, department store, had gotten on a bus at Court Square and taken a seat behind the white section of the bus. When the bus filled up, the driver ordered Mrs. Parks to stand and give up her seat to a white man. She refused to move. Two patrolmen took her to the local police station and booked her for violating the city bus ordinance.

Unwittingly, they were inviting a federal court test of the Jim Crow statutes on which the entire superstructure of segregation depended. The local courts, as expected, found against Mrs. Parks. This precipitated the "Miracle of Montgomery"—what King called the bus boycott that ultimately changed the law regarding blacks having to sit in the back of the bus and made Martin Luther King Jr. a household name.

In true symbolic frame fashion, King preached the cleansing of one's own house first. "They say we smell. No one is too poor to buy a bar of soap. They say we kill and cut each other," he said. In New York, Negroes constituted 10 percent of the population at that time and accounted for 35 percent of the crime. Blacks needed to correct this, King declared. "They say we speak poorly," he said. "You don't need to speak good English in order to be good," he asserted (Oates 1982, 126). He also disdained the use of Cadillacs and other big cars as a symbol to his followers that he and they should not feed the stereotype.

King did not see himself as the "Messiah" as some claimed, but he did have a sense of destiny. He saw himself as an instrument of history—of

God—and was very earnest about finding and doing his duty. And he went about spreading the word in a mostly symbolic way. His first book, *Stride Toward Freedom: The Montgomery Story*, was partly the story of the bus boycott, partly an autobiography, and partly an argument for nonviolence and racial change.

He was determined to carry out his mission using as much symbolism as he could muster. King told his wife, Coretta, and some friends that the time had come when he should no longer accept bail. If he committed a crime in the name of civil rights, he would go to jail and serve his time—in effect be a martyr for the cause. He was determined to give himself entirely as an example to his followers. So, at his trials, he stood up and spoke about his obligation and responsibility to no longer accept bail or pay the fines, but instead to go to prison.

King routinely handed these self-convictions to the startled judges and had Ralph Abernathy distribute copies to the newsmen. It was brilliant theater in the symbolic frame leadership tradition.

King professed indifference to material things and tried to imitate Gandhi. He drove around in a dusty three-year-old Chevrolet and only accepted $1 per year as SCLC president. He donated almost $230,000 from his speeches one year to the SCLC.

King deplored his father's deliberate approach toward desegregation. He was frustrated with all the delays and once scolded his father for not doing more in those years to challenge Atlanta's segregated facilities. He was different from his father in that way—he wanted to be free immediately. Always cognizant of the effect of symbolic frame behavior, he chose *We Shall Overcome*, an old labor union song, to become the hymn of the Negro Movement. He implored his followers to follow the "Montgomery Way" and not strike back at whites who shoved and screamed at them, but to be persistent, nevertheless (Oates 1986).

However, as we have seen, King was not always successful in his campaigns. An example was the unsuccessful Albany Movement in Albany, Georgia, in 1961 and 1962, where divisions within the black community and the nuanced, low-key response by local government officials defeated his efforts. But even in the midst of this ineffective use of symbolic frame behavior, King used even more symbolic frame leadership behavior to overcome the original setback.

In particular, King conducted the Birmingham Campaign to make up for the debacle in Albany and to show the nation that the SCLC could win victory for the Negro and that nonviolence was not dead. Birmingham, Alabama, was known to be the cradle of the Confederacy—the most segregated city in the South. Through the campaign and through his famous "Letter from Birmingham Jail," written in 1963, he was able to make a passionate statement for his crusade for justice and get the movement back on track.

King often observed that the nonviolent approach would force his oppressors to commit their brutality openly—in the light of day—and, in true symbolic frame form, King made sure the rest of the world was looking. Birmingham was a good strategic choice because of the inflammatory personalities of both Police Chief Bull Connor and Governor George Wallace. One or both could be counted on to make a mistake in judgment with virtually the whole nation watching on television or on the front pages of newspapers.

During the Birmingham campaign, King's "Letter from Birmingham Jail" became a classic in protest literature. Believed by many to be the most eloquent and learned expression of the goals and philosophy of the nonviolent movement ever written, it was yet another display of symbolic frame leadership behavior. It urged white clergymen to join the cause on moral grounds and made it virtually impossible for them to refuse their support and still maintain their integrity as clergymen.

What happened next in Birmingham made movement history. At the urging of King's young aides, hundreds of high-school students swarmed into SCLC workshops at the churches, all raring to march. So did hundreds of their little brothers and sisters from the elementary schools. In just one Birmingham march, over nine hundred young people were arrested and jailed. Looking back on it, one Birmingham police official said, "How stupid could we be?" (Oates 1986, 233).

Finally, Bull Connor made his predictable mistake alluded to earlier. He stood in the midst of a protest march, cigar in mouth and sweaty straw hat on his head, giving orders to his men. Several policemen had German Shepherd police dogs, which growled and strained at their leashes. When the peaceful demonstrators refused to return to church, Connor bellowed, "Let 'em have it" (Oates 1986, 237).

With scores of reporters and television cameramen recording every moment, the firemen turned their hoses onto the protesters, knocking them down and ripping off their clothes—all of which ended up on the primetime news reports and became Birmingham's day of infamy. A few days later, Connor ordered his men to do the same thing and they flatly refused to obey his orders. Two weeks later, Birmingham gave in to King's demands—mission accomplished.

King continued to make frequent use of symbolic frame leadership behavior throughout his remarkable career. To get the civil rights legislation moving in Congress in the 1960s, King organized a march on Washington that drew more than 250,000 people where he gave his "I _still_ have a dream" speech. He ended it with the memorable words: "I still dream of that day when all of God's children, black men and white men, Jews and Gentiles, Protestants and Catholics, will be able to join hands and sing in the words of the old Negro spiritual, 'Free at last! Free at last! Thank God almighty, we are free at last!'"

In 1964, he won the Novel Peace Prize, which acted as a symbol for his devotion to nonviolence. And after President Kennedy's assassination, King took advantage of another opportunity to display his symbolic frame side when he declared: "No memorial oration or eulogy could more eloquently honor President Kennedy's memory than the earliest possible passage of the civil rights bill for which he fought so long" (Oates 1986, 274). To add to his symbolic frame aura, in 1964, King became the first American Negro to be named *Time*'s "Man of the Year."

Later in his life, King used symbolic frame leadership behavior in protesting the Vietnam War. He dramatically pointed out the disproportionate number of Negroes among the troops and the violation of the civil rights of the Vietnamese. He also came out in favor of China being admitted into the United Nations.

The use of symbolic frame leadership behavior by King occurred once again on August 26, 1966, at the Palmer House in Chicago, when Mayor Richard Daley and King sat down for two and a half hours with powerful municipal, labor, and business leaders, and reached what became known as the "Summit Agreement." According to its terms, Chicago's Commission on Human Rights would require real-estate brokers to post a summary of the city's open-housing policy; Chicago's savings and bankers' association agreed to lend money to qualified families regardless of race and agreed to a ban on any further "redlining."

King continued to use symbolic leadership behavior until he drew his last breath. The Memphis sanitation workers' strike, with protesters carrying signs reading, "I AM A MAN," was King's last significant campaign. Here were poor black garbage collectors, asking a racist city government for decent pay and seeking a place in the union movement, a movement that had improved the lot of millions of whites but until that time was closed to blacks.

King gave his last great speech, the "Mountaintop Speech," on April 3, 1968, at the Mason Temple in Memphis, where he virtually predicted his death a day later. "I don't know what will happen now. . . . But it really doesn't matter with me now, because I have been to the mountaintop. Like anybody, I would like to live a long life. . . . So I'm happy tonight. I'm not worried about anything. I'm not fearing any man. . . . I have a dream this afternoon that the brotherhood of man will become a reality. . . . Free at last, Free at Last, Thank God almighty, we are free at last" (Oates 1986, 470). King was assassinated the next day, on April 4, 1968.

Chapter 9

THE POLITICAL FRAME

Leaders operating out of the political frame clarify what they want and what they can get. Political leaders are realists above all. They never let what they want cloud their judgment about what is possible. They assess the distribution of power and interests. They are all about "making friends and influencing people." Needless to say, Martin Luther King Jr. made it a point to effectively utilize political frame leadership behavior.

In his very first position as pastor of Dexter Avenue Baptist Church in Montgomery, Alabama, King practiced political leadership behavior. He served as his parishioners' character witness in court, negotiated with whites on their behalf, and married and buried them. To keep harmony within civil rights ranks, King oftentimes hastened to the New York headquarters and had long talks with Roy Wilkins of the NAACP assuring him that SCLC's approach supported and supplemented theirs. He did the same with the leadership of CORE and the Urban League.

Inevitably, the SCLC's growth and dominance brought about conflicts with the NAACP, as competitive staffers took to demeaning one another. The SCLC called the NAACP a "black bourgeoisie club" and the NAACP staffers responded in kind. King abhorred such sniping. When former baseball star Jackie Robinson wrote him about it, King replied in typical political frame fashion, indicating that he had always stressed the need for cooperation between the two organizations and complemented the NAACP as "our chief civil rights organization. The job ahead is too great," he said, "and the days ahead too bright to be bickering in the darkness of jealousy, deadening competition and internal ego struggles" (Oates 1986, 158).

And he backed up his words with actions. King had dinner with the Freedom Riders, for example, when they came through Atlanta, but elected not to accompany them since CORE started the Freedom Ride campaign and should get the credit. He contented himself with playing a supportive role.

With King, being nonpolitical was political. For example, King refused to endorse any political candidate, even Kennedy or Johnson; as he repeatedly said, no white leader except Lincoln had ever given enough support to the Negroes' struggle to warrant their confidence. Moreover, "I feel that someone must remain in the position of non-alignment, so that he can look objectively at both parties and be the conscience of both—not the servant or master of either" (Oates 1986, 159). But when he thought it was in the best interest of the cause, King took a political stand. Though he never publicly endorsed Kennedy, for example, he did about everything short of it. In fact, a number of newspapers erroneously reported that he had indeed endorsed the senator from Massachusetts for president.

King never limited himself to civil rights in using the political clout that he had accumulated. For example, he felt so strongly about the Bay of Pigs invasion that he signed a major newspaper advertisement denouncing it. "I did it," he said, "because I am as concerned about international affairs as I am about the civil rights struggle" (Oates 1986, 173).

In another political maneuver, King sought to strengthen the SCLC's ties with organized labor, with which Negroes shared a community of interests. George Meany's AFL-CIO, the nation's most powerful labor organization, became one of his greatest supporters. "Negroes," King said, "found that the history of labor mirrors their own experience" (Oates 1986, 186).

At times, King used political frame behavior reluctantly, but use it he did. For example, two months after the Birmingham campaign, which moved the Kennedys to introduce a new civil rights bill in Congress, the word was spread by King's enemies, which included J. Edgar Hoover, that King himself was a communist and that he harbored other communists in the SCLC. Kennedy informed King that the cry of communism could wreck the civil rights bill and imperil the movement, so against his better judgment, King decided to release suspected communist Jack O'Dell from the SCLC and curtail the activities of another suspected party member, Stanley Levison. Thus, King used political frame leadership behavior to further his goals even when the use of it was personally repugnant (Oates 1982).

THE MORAL FRAME

The moral frame is my own contribution to situational leadership theory. In my view, the moral frame *completes* situational leadership theory. Without it, leaders could just as easily use their leadership skills in promoting evil as for promoting good. Leaders operating out of the moral frame are concerned about their obligations and responsibilities to their followers. Moral frame leaders use some type of moral compass to direct their behavior. They practice what has been described as servant leadership and leading with heart, and are concerned with those individuals and groups that are marginalized in their organizations and in society. In short, they are concerned about equality, fairness, and social justice.

As an ordained minister, King's life was dedicated to a moral cause—the teachings of Jesus Christ. His concern for civil rights was rooted in Christ's command to "love one another as I have loved you." He opposed the Vietnam War and world poverty not on a political but on a moral basis. He was also a disciple of Mahatma Gandhi, whose policy of nonviolence in pursuit of human rights was based on moral law. King clearly relied on a moral compass to direct his leadership behavior.

KEY IDEAS

Martin Luther King Jr. was definitely a disciple of situational leadership theory. He effectively modeled all five frames of leadership behavior. For example, he used the structural frame in establishing the SCLC as the vehicle through which he pursued his civil rights agenda. He used the human resource frame in dedicating his life to obtaining human rights for all, especially the most disadvantaged.

His numerous inspirational speeches are an indication of his able use of the symbolic frame of leadership, and his political maneuvering with presidents Kennedy and Johnson enabled him to create a positive political climate for the passage of civil rights legislation. Finally, we saw how he engaged in the moral frame by basing his leadership enactment on a moral code, namely the teachings of Jesus Christ.

In conclusion, it seems to me that the leadership principles espoused and practiced by Martin Luther King Jr. transcend such variables as location and culture and would be useful to leaders and aspiring leaders no matter on which part of the globe they live.

Chapter Ten

Pope St. John Paul II

The future starts today, not tomorrow.

—*Pope St. John Paul II*

Born Karol Józef Wojtyła in 1920 in Poland, Wojtyła took the name John Paul II upon being named Pope in 1976. John Paul II was an orphan by age twelve and was raised by relatives.

He attended Krakow's Jagiellonian University where he showed an interest in theater, poetry, and athletics. But his real desire was to become a priest. He completed his religious studies at a Krakow seminary and was ordained a priest in 1946.

After serving as a parish priest for ten years, John Paul II was ordained bishop of Ombi in 1958 and then archbishop of Krakow in 1964. He was granted the cardinal's hat by Pope Paul VI in 1967.

After serving as bishop and becoming a cardinal, John Paul II made history by becoming the first non-Italian pope in more than four centuries. Beginning in 1978, he traveled the world, visiting more than one hundred countries, far outdistancing his predecessors. In 1981, an assassin shot John Paul twice in Vatican City as his Popemobile was circling St. Peter's Square. He was able to recover from his injuries, however, and later famously visited his attacker's prison cell and forgave him.

Known as an archconservative in matters of Roman Catholic dogma, John Paul II took a hardline stance on artificial birth control, abortion, and the ordination of women. However, he was a great champion of human rights and was against the death penalty.

Many believe that Pope John Paul II's greatest accomplishment was his part in bringing about the demise of the Soviet Union. He and Ronald Reagan are considered by many to be the two external figures who most contributed to the ultimate defeat of communism as an effective form of government. John Paul II and Ronald Reagan worked very closely to bring about the final outcome.

After the turn of the millennium, John Paul's health began to decline. He visibly trembled at times and was rumored to have Parkinson's disease. He passed away on April 2, 2005, at his Vatican City residence. More than three million believers passed his casket in St. Peter's Basilica. After at least three miracles were attributed to him, he was canonized a saint on April 27, 2014 (Bernstein 1996).

SITUATIONAL LEADERSHIP ANALYSIS

Situational models of leadership differ from earlier trait and behavioral models in asserting that no single way of leading works in all situations. Rather, appropriate behavior depends on the circumstances at a given time. Effective managers diagnose the situation, identify the leadership style or behavior that will be most effective, and then determine whether they can implement the required style. As we shall see, although he could be very rigid about Roman Catholic dogma, it can readily be asserted that Pope Saint John Paul II was a situational leader who was able and willing to vary his leadership behavior depending on the situation.

Even though he was more comfortable in certain of the five leadership frames, Pope John Paul II was able to appropriately alter his behavior when necessary. Normally apolitical in his outlook, once he decided that he would have to get involved in politics after all, he became a master at it. Jacek Woźniakowski, a leading spokesman for lay Catholics in Poland, said of John Paul II, "I was struck by what a quick study he was, how rapidly he assimilated information, how he reshaped it to his way of thinking, and how especially after following a long political discussion in silence, he had this extremely interesting way of summing things up" (Bernstein 1996, 124).

After returning from a successful visit to Mexico, John Paul II found himself face to face with a Kremlin elder and a member of the Politburo, Andrei Gromyko, the Soviet foreign minister. Gromyko was a stiff, glacial man, intelligent to be sure, but used to masking his thoughts with soulless bureaucratese. Any observation or objection bounced off him without prompting the slightest reaction, except for a few propagandistic clichés. John Paul II realized that his charm was useless here, but true to the situational nature of his leadership behavior, he adopted a very formal manner as he studied the man from Moscow.

On a visit to Poland, his homeland, his arrival at the national sanctuary at Czestochowa for a three-day stay coincided with a change of tone in his speeches. Religious themes now took over from political ones, though critical allusions to the communist system continued. In the wake of two recent labor strikes launched in Warsaw, John Paul II had chosen to intervene in a quieter voice, turning his many meetings with all sorts of citizens from the previously inflammatory ones into a "living catechism."

Because of John Paul II's reliance on situational leadership behavior, his papacy can be seen as three distinct phases in which he varied his leadership behavior depending on the primary goal of each phase. The first phase was the reestablishment of the church as a universal influence for good in the world. His foreign visits were the primary vehicle for addressing this goal.

The second phase was his battle against communism, in which he used mostly political frame leadership behavior. *Veritas Splendor*, published in the fifteenth year of his pontificate, is the encyclical of his maturity. In it he confronts what he considered the greatest danger in modern times: moral relativism.

Thus, in the third phase of his reign, the problem was the moral crisis of Western democracy. The pope believed that freedom has to be related to truth. Democracy without truth is doomed to fail, he declared. In the later years of his papacy, issues such as materialism, secularism, abortion, and human rights were his focus, and he mainly used structural frame leadership in the form of using papal encyclicals to make his points.

THE STRUCTURAL FRAME

Structural frame leaders seek to develop a new model of the relationship of structure, strategy, and environment for their organizations. Strategic planning, extensive preparation, and effecting change are priorities for them. John Paul II was very astute at practicing structural frame leadership behavior under the proper circumstances.

When John Paul II was challenged theologically or philosophically, one could readily see his structural frame behavior come to the surface. He would firmly stand his ground, but in a loving way. To him, others have to be lovingly led by the hand, like children, onto the path of truth, which they will then come to see for themselves. On issues like contraception, abortion, women priests, gay marriage, divorce, and the like, he would take a structural frame leadership approach and immediately go into his teaching mode, but with a human resource touch.

According to Cardinal Jean Villot, John Paul II's secretary of state, one's first impression of the pope was of his care for humanity. But there was an aspect of his personality that did not reveal itself at first blush, a hard, hidden core that sustained him, an iron will and an unlimited belief in the power of that will. "It is through the will that man is lord of his actions," John Paul II noted in one of his essays, adding that self-control is the most fundamental manifestation of the value of a person (Bernstein 1996, 121). Anyone who ignored his winning smile and instead looked him straight in the eye would have known that there was structural frame leadership enactment at his core.

One of the first things that John Paul II did as pope was to use structural frame behavior and expound on his policies and strategies: fidelity to the Vatican Council above all, and collegiality—those were the issues close to the heart of those who did not wish to give up on Church renewal. And then, as requested by the majority of the cardinals, who were frightened by the all too rapid changes of the postcouncil period, John Paul II insisted on obedience to the pope's teaching, respect for liturgical rules, and discipline. Finally, he stressed the need to carry on the ecumenical dialogue and reiterated the Church's commitment to peace and justice in the world. This was exactly the program that got him elected.

He further exhorted the clergy in Rome not to water down their priestly charism with exaggerated interest in social problems. He championed the cause of celibacy as the best way to devote one's energies exclusively to the priestly goal of leading one's followers to salvation. He invited the American bishops to keep a watchful eye on Christian doctrine and church discipline.

At a conference with nuns, he insisted on the necessity of wearing the religious habit. He reminded members of the Vatican Secretariat for the Union of Christians that the ecumenical movement could not make progress by compromising the truth. He extolled mothers who refused to have abortions when their lives were at risk. He reaffirmed the indissolubility of marriage and forbade dialogue regarding the ordination of women.

In his negotiations with communist states, John Paul II utilized structural frame leadership behavior frequently, instructing his representatives that henceforth in their bargaining with the communist states, they should not minimize the irreconcilability of Marxism with the truth. Rather, they should highlight it.

To the recalcitrant clergy supporting liberation theology, mostly in Central and South America, the pope hammered away, urging them not to be swayed by alluring calls to political commitment. "You are spiritual guides, not social leaders, not political executives or functionaries of a secular order," he said. His Polish experience taught him not to align the Church with any political party or ideology. "This notion," he proclaimed, "is not in harmony with the Church's teaching" (Bernstein 1996, 209).

In true structural frame leadership style, he sent an unequivocal message to the Latin Americans and a crystal-clear signal that immediately got through to the Kremlin and the White House. The pope from Krakow would never let Catholics align themselves with Marxist movements—or capitalistic ones for that matter—in a battle for social justice and democracy.

The Polish pope would never approve of what the Italian Pope Paul VI had declared in his encyclical *Populorum Progresso*—permission in extreme cases to revolt against deeply entrenched dictatorships. The Polish youth, who under Krakow's Nazi occupation had prayed for deliverance but had never joined the resistance, was now imposing his methods on the clergy and the church.

Pope John Paul II used structural frame behavior in his efforts to overthrow the Communist Party in his native Poland. The labor strikes that occurred at the shipyards there were just the opening that the pope sought. Part of his strategy for defeating communism was to take advantage of any sign of a chink in communism's armor, so he publicly endorsed the strikes.

In a typical structural frame leadership move, John Paul II planned to use Zbigniew Brzezinski, the Polish-born national security advisor of Jimmy Carter and Ronald Reagan, in his assault on communism. After the initial stage was set through Brzezinski, John Paul II planned to use Reagan himself as his primary partner in the process. Reagan and the pope agreed with Brzezinski's assessment: "If you were able to shake and disrupt Poland, then the shock waves would radiate out in many directions, into the Ukraine, the Balkans, in Latvia, Lithuania and Estonia, and Czechoslovakia" (Bernstein 1996, 262).

The pope's strategy in his fight with Soviet communism and the Polish government's imposition of martial law was for the Polish labor movement, Solidarity, to remain alive underground, to resume publishing and broadcasting, and to somehow, through the Church and through his own person, rally the spirits of the people when the time was right. With that in mind, the pope began secretly sending money from papal discretionary funds to Solidarity and planning his own trip to Poland, which, before the imposition of martial law, had been scheduled for August 1982. He had to delay his visit until 1983, but soon after the visit, it was no coincidence that martial law was lifted and the Communist Party's influence in Poland began to wane.

Pope John Paul II further exhibited structural frame behavior in his daily work schedule. Leaving his bedroom with its modest single bed and two straight-back upholstered chairs, the pope began his seventeen-hour workday. Unlike many of his predecessors, John Paul II took his responsibilities as bishop of Rome seriously. On Sundays, he often visited one of the 323 Roman parish churches. The week before the visits, John Paul II would invite the pastors to the Vatican to hear about the problems of his parish and his parishioners.

As a practicing structural frame leader, Pope John Paul II always kept his primary goals in sight. Whether in the Vatican or on his travels, everything he did was aimed at building support for his leadership and his vision of a Catholic Church with no inferiority complex vis-à-vis modern society. As pope, he demanded that, first and foremost, the Church's leaders, priests, nuns, bishops, prelates, and theologians obey papal teachings such as celibacy, staying out of politics, administering the sacraments, wearing religious garb, and so on.

When John Paul II sensed that the Church was moving away from traditional doctrine, he, under the guise of fulfilling the recommendations of Vatican II, called the Great Synod in 1986, which was a meeting held in Rome of representatives, both lay and clergy, from all over the world. The pope was quite satisfied with the report of the synod as well as the bishops' approval of it. His intention was to institute reforms in the Church without shaking the structure and theological underpinnings handed down through the ages. "The synod," he announced to the bishops, "had done a good job" (Bernstein 1996, 438).

During his papacy, conciliar reforms (i.e., Vatican II reforms), however modest, spread throughout the Church and were realized in the daily practice of many Catholic communities, including a modernized liturgy; improved relations with members of Protestant, Orthodox, and Jewish faiths; more frequent consultation between the Vatican and the bishops; increased roles for girls and women in the Mass and other religious ceremonies; and the presentation of the Church as a community, not just a hierarchical, monarchical society. However, as is oftentimes characteristic of a structural frame leader, the basic doctrine and practice remained very firmly intact (Bernstein 1996).

THE HUMAN RESOURCE FRAME

Human resource leaders believe in people and communicate that belief. They are passionate about productivity through people. There are myriad instances of Pope John Paul II expressing his respect for human dignity through the practice of human resource frame leadership behavior.

John Paul II often expressed human resource frame behavior in his ecumenical practices. For instance, Jurek Kluger, his Jewish boyhood friend, once ran into the parish church to get Karol to join him in a soccer game, to the amazement of the women who saw the son of the president of the Jewish community next to the altar. John Paul II remarked, "Aren't we all God's children?" (Bernstein 1996, 32).

He reinforced his position toward non-Christians after he become pope, when he declared that "the cause of Christ can also be furthered by the choice of a worldview diametrically opposed to Christianity. Everyone who makes this choice with the innermost conviction must have our respect" (Bernstein 1996, 224).

As mentioned earlier, Pope John Paul II especially loved young people. They were his hope and the future of the Church. For them he established World Youth Day in 1986, a biannual pilgrimage in Europe, Asia, or the

Americas attended by hundreds of thousands of young Catholics from around the world, over which he presided for days of masses, processions, homilies, and workshops. He expressed what he referred to as an "authentic fatherhood" toward them.

Perhaps the following incident best demonstrates John Paul II's reliance on human resource frame leadership behavior even in uncomfortable situations. A young student body president at Louvain-la-Neuve, Veronique Yoruba, verbally attacked the pope about his stand on the sinfulness of contraception. Her question generated an audience outburst, with John Paul II fans and Yoruba fans taunting one another. John Paul II's reaction was mild and paternal—he simply kissed the young student on the head (Bernstein 1996).

THE SYMBOLIC FRAME

In the symbolic frame, the organization is seen as a stage, a theater in which every actor plays certain roles, and the symbolic leader attempts to communicate the right impressions to the right audiences. Considering John Paul II's experience onstage as a young actor, it is not surprising that as pope he was extremely active in the symbolic frame.

We begin the exploration of John Paul II's extensive use of symbolic frame leadership enactments in 1986 when the Polish Communist Party leaders in Warsaw, under pressure from the hawks in the Kremlin, East Berlin, and Prague, had refused permission for John Paul II's visit to Poland. After the decision was reversed, the pope finally made his triumphant journey to his homeland. Now history was taking its revenge.

Like a smiling nemesis, Pope John Paul II was knocking on Poland's proverbial door. He was returning to his own country like a conqueror, and, although the communist leaders could not have known it yet, in the future he would come back anytime he wished. With the support of the vast majority of the people of Poland, the pope was now in the driver's seat.

For the next nine days during his first visit to Poland as pope, the men, women, and especially the young people of Poland would live in a sort of hypnotic trance of sustained excitement, as if they were experiencing not just a visit of a compatriot who had assumed supreme religious authority over one of the world's great faiths, but the coming of an emperor, a messiah. The experience was overwhelming and irresistible.

What was taking place at Warsaw's Victory Square was a breakthrough to unknown horizons. In true symbolic form, John Paul II never uttered a word that might lead directly to a confrontation between church and state, between the Communist Party and Christian believers, but everything he said marked the beginning of a grand turnabout for the Church in Poland, in

Eastern Europe, in the Soviet Union, and in world affairs. Through him, the Church was laying claim to a new role, no longer simply asking space for itself. Through him, it was demanding respect for human rights as well as for Christian values, respect for every man and woman, and respect for the autonomy of the individual. These demands, of course, represented a direct assault on Marxist ideology.

At the same time, in the United States, Ronald Reagan was campaigning for the Republican presidential nomination. He was said to be sitting in front of a little portable television on the veranda of his ranch near Santa Barbara with Richard Allen, a Catholic, who would become his first national security advisor. As the crowd around John Paul II dispersed, Reagan's eyes began to fill with tears. What the two men were witnessing confirmed that there was a cancer spreading in the body of communism (Bernstein 1996, 8).

"How many divisions has the pope?" Stalin asked contemptuously during World War II. To this question, an answer would soon be given. John Paul II was both the inspiration for and the ultimate protector of the Solidarity movement, a noncommunist Polish workers' alliance within the Soviet empire that eventually would help free Poland from Russian domination. With the Solidarity movement at his side, he had what amounted to many divisions, indeed.

The pope's confrontation with communism took place in the context not of a specific religious denomination or ideological issue, but of the rights of man, pure and simple. John Paul II's ascension to the papal throne and the ensuing events in Poland were redrawing the strategic map of the Cold War. For decades, it had been axiomatic that Moscow and Washington were the essential coordinates, with Berlin the critical point between. Now, like a painting being completed, two other key points came into the picture: the Vatican and Warsaw.

John Paul II saw himself as a man called by God to change the face of his church and the world. He had been an actor, poet, playwright, and philosopher—and now a pontiff. What was somewhat surprising was the skill he employed as a politician on the world's stage. As pope, he became one of the most remarkable figures of the second half of the twentieth century. Though a mystic and solitary by nature, he was energized during his many papal visits by some of the largest crowds in history ever assembled before a leader.

I had the opportunity to witness firsthand the characteristic charisma of John Paul II. In 1979, as cochair of the Papal Visit Committee that organized the pope's visit to Philadelphia, and again a couple of years later when I attended the opening mass at the New Orleans Superdome when he visited there, I saw how the young people greeted the pontiff with the kind of mass hysteria that was usually reserved for rock superstars. His ability to effectively utilize symbolic leadership behavior was nonpareil.

Even as a young Polish cardinal, John Paul II knew the impact of symbolic behavior. For example, from his earliest days as a bishop, he had tried to obtain a building permit for a long-promised church at Nowa Huta, the vast new industrial quarter built by the communists in Krakow. So he spent Christmas Eve celebrating midnight mass outdoors in the snow and subzero cold at the site where the regime had reneged on its promise.

John Paul II had a boldness that was very different from the practiced reserve of Pope Paul VI and the smiling timidity of Pope John Paul I, his predecessor. Here was someone who wanted to shake the church out of its doldrums in regard to its place in the world. John Paul II spoke with a professional's rhythmic intonation, measuring the pauses and breaking off for moments of applause. In a sense, he was the supreme showman.

John Paul II's use of symbolic frame leadership behavior began as early as his very first trip abroad as pope. He decided to make his first trip to countries outside of Europe that had a longstanding Roman Catholic tradition—Mexico and South America. However, Cardinal Jean Villot, the pope's secretary of state, was alarmed for the pontiff while visiting these anticlerical countries.

Villot was afraid the pope would not be received with the honors due to his rank. But John Paul II was not interested in the qualms of his secretary of state or in the niceties of protocol. What he had in mind was something foreign to any Vatican bureaucrat, something as revolutionary as the Vatican Council itself—the remaking of the papacy for Christianity's third millennium—and thus he became the most traveled pontiff in history.

As it happened, the Mexican people paid no attention to these political barriers. Their profoundly Catholic faith swept away the question of whether in bygone days the church had sided with the aristocracy. All the church bells in the city were ringing. At the airport, as a little orchestra played a papal welcome, the crowd broke the police lines and surged around the pope. Millions of Mexicans occupied the route to Mexico City's central square, waving thousands of little white-and-yellow papal flags. This scene was duplicated innumerable times as John Paul II visited more than one hundred countries during his long papacy.

One of his predecessors, Paul VI, took only eight foreign trips in his fifteen years as pope. By comparison, in his first six years alone, John Paul II visited thirty-seven foreign countries in his attempt to demonstrate that the church was truly universal. As often as not, he visited parts of the world where human beings lived in impoverished conditions of oppression, illness, and hunger. He gave them a voice. He also wanted to assert his own place in global leadership. It was his great charism, more than his doctrinal message, that was most formidable for keeping the Church together.

In front of the camera, his global evangelization came to life. He was the first pope to understand the television era and master the medium. Liturgies celebrated by the pope became epic performances. Wherever he appeared in cities, a Super Bowl atmosphere prevailed.

John Paul II's visit to Auschwitz was particularly symbolic. The bishop of Rome knelt down and looked at the cement floor of the death cell. He had with him a small bouquet of white and red carnations, which he placed delicately on the ground. Then he bent down to kiss the same slab of concrete on which the Franciscan priest Father Maximilian Kolbe had lain in agony. Of course some Jews were upset because he only honored a Catholic's martyrdom. They completely missed the intended point that the pope was both honoring the martyred Jews and apologizing for past anti-Jewish sentiments promoted by the Catholic Church by being the first pope to visit a site of the tragic Holocaust.

Along with political frame leadership behavior, Pope John Paul II utilized symbolic frame leadership behavior in his war on communism. While the pope worked in his study on plans to defeat communism, Lech Wałęsa, with the pope's encouragement, was climbing onto a steam shovel at the Lenin Shipyard in Gdansk, Poland, urging the workers to unite.

On August 31, 1976, the historic Gdansk accords were signed, ratifying the establishment of the first independent labor union behind the Iron Curtain. It was the beginning of the end of communism in Poland and eventually in the entire Soviet bloc. And the symbolism of the Gdansk accords did not go unnoticed throughout the world. Sister Zofia Zdybicka, a philosopher friend of John Paul II, while watching the strikes on television news, said, "This is a lesson for the whole world. Look at the contradiction: The *workers* are against communism" (Bernstein 1996, 241).

Further use of symbolic frame leadership enactments took place in John Paul II's relationship with Ronald Reagan in their mutual efforts to defeat communism. Although they were political opposites, the pope and Ronald Reagan did find common ground. Both had been actors. Neither was moved quickly to anger. Both believed in the power of the symbolic act as well as in the role of divine Providence, particularly after both had been shot by assassins within six weeks of each other and had survived. In the first minutes of their first meeting, both agreed that they had been saved by God to play a special role in the destiny of Eastern Europe. "Look at the evil forces that were put in our way and how Providence intervened," Reagan said. The pope agreed (Bernstein 1996, 357).

Visiting his would-be assassin, Mehmet Ali Agca, in prison served both a symbolic and a political purpose. It was symbolic because the pope was reflecting Christ's forgiveness, and political because the pope was sending a message to the Soviets, who many believed were responsible, that he was forgiving them for whatever complicity they may have had in the attempted assassination because not doing so would have seriously set back efforts toward defeating communism and bringing about world peace and would have put the Soviet Union in a dangerously isolated international position.

Pope John Paul II also had a symbolic purpose in creating many new saints during his tenure. He wished to point out the fecundity of the church, like a father proudly showing off his children. Among other things, saints are symbols of a flourishing religious life, role models for their cultures and communities, and a stimulus for overcoming sagging priestly vocations. Sometimes John Paul II favored overtly political canonizations, like those members of religious orders killed in the Mexican and French Revolutions or the Spanish Civil War. He saw them as symbolic victims of the evil produced by bloody revolutions or by anticlerical and Marxist regimes.

In 1986, John Paul II partook in yet another display of symbolic frame leadership behavior when he went to India to pray at the tomb of Mahatma Gandhi in New Delhi. Encouraged by his reception in India, he developed the idea of holding an international, interreligious assembly in Assisi, the birthplace of St. Francis, the most peace-loving and joyful of the Christian saints, to pray for world peace in another grand gesture of his pontificate. At the first assembly on October 27, 1986, combatants momentarily held a ceasefire in many countries around the world.

Finally, in 1986, the Berlin Wall came down, and the communist satellites began to fall. On December 1, 1989, the sidewalks of the great avenue leading to the Vatican were filled with tens of thousands in a state of anticipation and excitement. The general secretary of the Communist Party of the Soviet Union and the supreme pontiff of the Roman Catholic Church were about to meet for the first time in history (Bernstein 1996).

THE POLITICAL FRAME

Leaders operating out of the political frame clarify what they want and what they can get. Political leaders are realists above all. They never let what they want cloud their judgment about what is possible. They assess the distribution of power and interests. They are primarily concerned with "making friends and influencing people." Although he dissuaded his priests from running for office or endorsing any particular political party, John Paul II himself heavily engaged in political frame leadership behavior.

Recognizing John Paul II's potential for engaging in effective political frame leadership enactments, Soviet foreign minister Andrei Gromyko constantly warned his colleagues in the Kremlin not to underestimate John Paul II's ability to stir up the Polish masses the way Khomeini had incited the Iranian people. Gromyko proved correct when the pope met William Casey, a practicing Catholic who was a daily communicant and the director of the US Central Intelligence Agency. Casey handed over to John Paul II a remarkable photograph taken by one of America's spy satellites. It was of John Paul II addressing his compatriots in Victory Square in 1979. Casey used the photo to help seal an informal secret alliance between the Holy See and the administration of Ronald Reagan. These two men met perhaps a half dozen times in an alliance that would see communism collapse, first in the pope's homeland of Poland, then in Eastern Europe, and finally in the Soviet Union itself.

Even as archbishop of Krakow, John Paul II became increasingly convinced that the Communist Party would not be able to continue to maintain hegemonic power in society, so he began to exploit this fact to the church's advantage. He flooded the Soviet authorities with petitions and requests for new seminaries, churches, and public processions. He protested the government's attempt to prevent the teaching of the catechism to children; he demanded respect for the provisions of the 1950 accord between the church and the state, which exempted seminaries from the draft; and he fought to affirm the freedom of Christians to practice their faith without enduring intimidation.

But before utilizing political frame behavior to help defeat communism, the pope grew confident in using it in the administration of his papal duties within his own flock. After Vatican II, the Catholic bishops of the world wanted a greater share in the decision making within the church. John Paul II resolved the problem of power sharing by the passive-aggressive behavior of first suggesting a special committee to consider the question and then, before the committee even formed, establishing a new entity like the Synod of Bishops as a consultative body. John Paul II adopted this political frame style from his predecessor, Pope Paul VI, who was extremely adept at alternating measures that placated the traditionalist minority and encouraged the reformist majority.

So John Paul II was well versed in the use of political frame leadership behavior by the time he took on the Soviet Union. At first he used political behavior more subtly and later more forcibly. For example, during a visit to Poland in the midst of the imposition of martial law in reaction to the labor strikes throughout the country, the pope decided to use political frame behavior to acknowledge that, although he disagreed with the communist ideology, he respected the Russian people.

"Once again I choose to stop at another memorial stone [in a military cemetery], this one in Russian," he said. "I will not add any comments. We know what country it speaks of. We are aware of the past played by this country in the last terrible war for the freedom of the nations." This was the gesture the government in Warsaw had been seeking, the conciliatory sign to Moscow. The pope, however, was careful in his words, saying "Russians," not "Soviets" (Bernstein 1996, 229).

The labor strikes that shook Poland in the summer of 1980, and which were supported by the pope, were not merely strikes. They were political insurrections—counterinsurrections, as Leonid Brezhnev described them. This movement, like many historic social revolutions, united almost the entire constellation of formidable political forces—labor, the intellectuals, and the church—that had never before come together so decisively.

The beginning of negotiations to end the strikes in exchange for various concessions, turned into a dramatic weeklong test of wills. A group of advisors, two of whom were close associates of John Paul II, joined Lech Wałęsa in the negotiations. The group came to be known as Solidarity. The strong stance in favor of Solidarity by John Paul II helped resolve the Polish crisis. Through the exercise of political frame leadership behavior, the pope's will had become the national will of Poland. Now the communist government had little choice but to give in to the unions' demands.

Throughout the Polish crisis that would dominate the first decade of his papacy, the pope sought a delicate balance—how to simultaneously support the workers and destroy communism, but avoid the bloodbath that he feared if the Soviets were to join the Polish communists in putting down the unions by force.

John Paul II, as mentioned earlier, had a powerful ally in the process of overcoming communism, in the person of Ronald Reagan. Cardinal John Krol of Philadelphia introduced Reagan to the pope and acted as an intermediary between the two. Being a friend of both, he convinced John Paul II that Reagan was sincere, even though he represented a capitalistic and materialistic society of which the pope was suspicious. Thus Krol was in a position to do what no other prince of the church could do—convince John Paul II that the interests of Poland, the Vatican, and the United States were in concert—and to overcome whatever reservations the pope had about forming such a close relationship with the American president.

Even though the pope was suspicious of the excesses of capitalism and materialism in the United States, he never once criticized the Reagan administration. In fact, when the Vatican Academy of Sciences prepared a report sharply critical of Reagan's Strategic Defense Initiative, dubbed "Star Wars" by the media, the pope used political frame leadership behavior and had it buried. His primary goal was to rid the world of communism, and he knew he had an ally in Reagan, and not until the Persian Gulf War in 1991—after the fall of communism in Eastern and Central Europe—did the pope publicly oppose a single major feature of American policy.

The advent of Mikhail Gorbachev brought rapid changes to church–state relations in Poland and created an atmosphere in which the pope could more effectively use political frame leadership behavior and be influential in Poland's dropping of martial law, not to mention communism. John Paul II and

Gorbachev were both Slavs and could relate to one another. As we have seen, the Pope took full advantage of the circumstances (Bernstein 1996).

THE MORAL FRAME

The moral frame is my own contribution to situational leadership theory. In my view, the moral frame completes situational leadership theory. Without it, leaders could just as easily use their leadership skills for promoting evil as for promoting good. Leaders operating out of the moral frame are concerned about their obligations and responsibilities to their followers. Moral frame leaders use some type of moral compass to direct their behavior. They practice what has been described as servant leadership and are concerned with those individuals and groups that are marginalized in their organizations and in society. In short, they are concerned about equality, fairness, and social justice.

It is obvious that Pope John Paul II utilized the moral frame as an integral aspect of his overall leadership behavior. At his ordination to the Catholic priesthood, he took an oath to model his life after that of Jesus Christ and the Gospels. Thus, the life of Christ and the Gospels served as John Paul II's moral compass, giving direction to his leadership behavior.

KEY IDEAS

There is no question that Pope St. John Paul II was a situational leader. We saw how he was active in all five frames of leadership, depending on the situation. Most likely due to his experience as an actor, his forte seems to have been the symbolic frame. He had a charismatic personality that enabled him to attract huge and enthusiastic crowds to the events in which he participated. Leaders and potential leaders have much to learn by examining and internalizing his leadership principles.

Perhaps John Paul II's greatest achievement was his part in the defeat of communism. He, along with his friend and collaborator Ronald Reagan, is commonly credited with having the most to do with the ultimate victory. Of course Mikhail Gorbachev presented them with the opportunity because of his openness to change. Nevertheless, we have seen how John Paul II effectively utilized situational leadership principles in his efforts to overthrow communism in the Soviet Union.

Chapter Eleven

St. Mother Teresa

A beautiful death is for people who lived like animals to die like angels—loved and wanted.

— *St. Mother Teresa*

St. Mother Teresa of Calcutta was born in 1910 in Albania. At the age of eighteen, she left home to join the Sisters of Loreto as a missionary. She had served as a teacher at the Loreto convent school in Calcutta for twenty years when she experienced a "calling" to continue her ministry in the service of the poor. She began her missionary work with the poor in 1948, replacing her Loreto habit with the internationally familiar simple white sari with a blue border. This habit became the symbol of the Missionaries of Charity, a religious order that she founded in 1950.

Her congregation, which was chartered to minister to the hungry, the naked, the homeless, the crippled, the blind, the lepers, and all those who had become a burden to society began as a small order with thirteen members in the city of Calcutta. By 1997, it had grown to more than four thousand sisters in charity centers worldwide. In 1963, she founded the Missionaries of Charity Brothers for men who wished to dedicate their lives to the poor. In 1976, she founded a contemplative branch of the Missionaries of Charity.

Mother Teresa was the recipient of numerous honors and awards, including the 1979 Nobel Peace Prize. She was named in the yearly Gallup poll of the world's most admired men or women eighteen times and became one of the most recognizable women in the world. She suffered a heart attack in Rome in 1983, and after several other heart attacks, a broken collarbone, and numerous bouts of malaria, she died in 1997. Her beatification by Pope John Paul II following her death gave her the title "Blessed Teresa of Calcutta." In 2016, Pope Francis canonized her as a saint in the Roman Catholic Church (Spink 1997).

Chapter 11

SITUATIONAL LEADERSHIP ANALYSIS

There is not much doubt but that Mother Teresa manifested many of the characteristics associated with situational, transformational female leaders such as being concerned with emotions, values, ethics, standards, and long-term goals and engaging with others in creating a connection that raises the level of motivation and morality in both herself and her followers. Furthermore, she satisfied her followers' needs, and treated them like full human beings as well as empowering them and nurturing them in the process of change In sum, she utilized situational leadership theory in establishing a vision, building the capacities of her followers, and fostering collaborative and democratic participation in change.

THE STRUCTURAL FRAME

Structural frame leaders seek to develop a new model of the relationship of structure, strategy, and environment for their organizations. Strategic planning, extensive preparation, and effecting change are priorities for them. Mother Teresa was very astute at practicing structural frame leadership behavior under the proper circumstances.

Thus, we begin our analysis of Mother Teresa's leadership behavior with the structural frame. Examples of Mother Teresa's use of the structural frame abound. "What Mother wants, she gets" was a truism widely accepted among those who knew her. Small notes written by hand and signed *Mother* gave directions relating to the most ordinary of practical details. The central courtyard of the motherhouse contained two tanks of water. "Sisters, please do not keep anything on top of the tank," a carefully handwritten note commanded (Spink 1997, ix). Through the astute use of structural frame leadership behavior, Mother Teresa was able to spread her Sisters of Charity congregation to an astounding five hundred branches throughout the world.

Mother Teresa's directions to her sisters were those of a firm believer in discipline; obedience was to be "prompt, simple, blind and cheerful, for Jesus was obedient unto death." Charity was to be manifested in "words, deeds, thoughts, desires and feelings, for Jesus went about doing good." Poverty was to be applied to all "desires and attachments, in likes and dislikes, for Jesus being rich made himself poor for us." Chastity was to be lived "in thoughts and affections, in desires and attachments, for Jesus is a jealous lover" (Spink 1997, 73).

By 1979, only fifteen years after their founding, there were 158 Sisters of Charity foundations scattered throughout the world, 1,187 professed sisters, 411 novices, and 120 postulants—and many more to come. Again utilizing structural frame leadership behavior, Mother Teresa established the Missionary Brothers of Charity in 1967. She rationalized the foundation of a male order by noting that "you can do what I can't do. I can do what you can't do. Together we can do something beautiful for God" (Spink 1997, 103).

Mother Teresa showed her structural frame side in dealing with a priest who had disdained the traditional beliefs held by Mother Teresa and her congregation, among which was genuflecting before the Blessed Sacrament, what Catholics believe is the body and blood of Jesus Christ. He said there was no need to do so outside of the Mass. After he had finished speaking, Mother Teresa led the priest to the door, thanked him for coming, and informed him that he need not come again. She then proceeded to refute everything he had said in an hour-long discourse with her nuns.

THE HUMAN RESOURCE FRAME

Human resource leaders believe in people and communicate that belief. They are passionate about productivity through people. It is through the use of the human resource frame that leaders typically express their emotional intelligence.

As far as the use of the human resource frame was concerned, Mother Teresa was quite prolific. After all, she dedicated her very being to the service of the poor. Like her role model Mahatma Gandhi, Mother Teresa considered every person to be a reflection of God. "Every person is Christ for me," she often said. "Since there is only one Jesus, the person I am meeting is the one person in the world at that moment." She was equally concerned about the unborn, as she set about combating abortion with adoption. She sent word out to the hospitals and clinics, "Please do not destroy the child. We will take the child" (Spink 1997, 62).

Every morning, Mother Teresa would go from one tiny body to the next in her children's home in Calcutta. If she spotted one who was so frail and sick that he or she seemed likely to die that day, Mother Teresa would wrap the child in a blanket and give it to one of her helpers to hold, with the simple instruction to love the child until the child died. Her concern for people went far beyond the poor. When Queen Elizabeth II presented her with the Honorary Order of Merit, Mother Teresa inquired, "And how is your grandson, Prince William?" (Spink 1997, 180).

THE SYMBOLIC FRAME

In the symbolic frame, the organization is seen as a stage, a theater in which every actor plays certain roles, and the symbolic frame leader attempts to communicate the right impressions to the right audiences.

Again in the fashion of her countryman Mahatma Gandhi, Mother Teresa practiced symbolic leadership behavior with great frequency. Both individuals were very cognizant of their images and were careful to cultivate and project behavior that would reflect their ideals. For example, Mother Teresa cultivated her image of humility by noting that "No one thinks of the pen while writing a letter. That's exactly what I am in God's hand—a little pencil" (Spink 1997, xii).

While Gandhi had his distinctive garb, Mother Teresa followed his lead by establishing her own unique uniform. In preparation for founding the Missionaries of Charity, she purchased three saris from the local bazaar—white ones edged with three blue stripes, which would in time become the distinctive habit of the new congregation. Symbolic frame behavior such as this was once again manifested when Mother Teresa was presented with the white Lincoln limousine that Pope Paul VI had used during his 1964 visit to India. Mother Teresa promptly raffled it off and used the proceeds for the poor.

In a similar incident in 1979, she earmarked the money she received for the Nobel Peace Prize for the hungry of Norway. The usual celebratory banquet was also canceled at her request, and again the money was used, with an additional amount raised by Norwegian young people, for the poor.

In preparation for Christmas at her motherhouse in Calcutta, Mother Teresa once again exhibited symbolic frame behavior by setting up an empty crib in the chapel. Also in the chapel was a box containing straw. The sisters were encouraged to make small personal sacrifices and then to discreetly take a piece of straw from the box and place it in the crib so that when the baby Jesus was laid in the manger on Christmas Day, it would be a crib warmed by their love and sacrifice.

As mentioned earlier, Mother Teresa was a great admirer of Mahatma Gandhi, although they never met. She called her new international association of lay workers the "Co-Workers of Mother Teresa," because that is how Gandhi referred to his followers. And, symbolically adhering to Gandhi's principles of nonviolence, she said, "Let us not use bombs and guns to overcome the world. Let us use love and compassion. Peace begins with a smile" (Spink 1997, 173).

In my own personal encounter with Mother Teresa at the 41st International Eucharistic Congress in 1976 in Philadelphia, she once again engaged in symbolic frame leadership behavior. Despite having a lavish luncheon available for her between speeches, she insisted on having only a bowl of soup in deference to the poor. Nevertheless, she was careful to thank those who prepared the more elaborate meal.

In a final example of Mother Teresa's frequent use of symbolic frame leadership behavior, she was criticized for giving the poor fish instead of teaching them how to fish. In response, she said, "Ah, my God, you should see these people. They have not even the strength to lift a fishing rod, let alone use it to fish. Giving them fish, I help them to recover the strength for their fishing of tomorrow."

She was similarly criticized by intellectuals for not having a cutting-edge philosophy that was tied to psychology and sociology. Once asked by a professor of sociology why she cared for people the way she did, she asked him if he had a flower garden. "Do you take care of the flowers?" she asked. "Don't you think a human being is so much more than a flower?" (Spink 1997, 186).

THE POLITICAL FRAME

Leaders operating out of the political frame clarify what they want and what they can get. Political leaders are realists above all. They never let what they want cloud their judgment about what is possible. They assess the distribution of power and interests. They are primarily concerned with "making friends and influencing people."

Like Gandhi, Mother Teresa engaged in political leadership behavior when necessary and appropriate. The municipality of Calcutta was seeking a solution to the public relations problem of the destitute dying in the streets, and there, quite unexpectedly, was a woman of considerable energy and determination offering to take care of them. When Mother Teresa applied to the municipality for a house, the municipality realized that in exchange for the gift of a house, Mother Teresa was offering to salve the consciences of Calcutta's more socially minded citizens.

On the occasion of former Indian president Indira Gandhi's public support for sterilization as a means of birth control, Mother Teresa went to the capitol to confront her. It was one of her rare attempts at intervention on a political issue, but this one she considered to be a moral question. Mother Teresa's power with the people became evident when, shortly after Indira Gandhi continued her support for sterilization, she was defeated at the polls and was succeeded by the prolife candidate.

In a similar incident, in reaction to the Freedom of Religion bill in India, which would discourage the activities of foreign, especially non-Hindu, missionaries, she wrote to parliament, saying, "After much prayer and sacrifices I write to you asking you to face God in prayer before you take a step which will destroy the joy and freedom of our people. Don't belittle our Hindu religion by saying that our Hindu people will give up their religion for a plate of rice" (Spink 1997, 157).

In 1985, at the invitation of the Patriotic Church in China (which was Catholic but not aligned with Rome), Mother Teresa finally set foot in China for the first time. Her particular gift for opening difficult doors was dramatically brought to light. She was by no means as politically naive or unfamiliar with the ways of the world as it sometimes suited her to appear. She was political by not being political. She knew she had an ability to draw out a chivalrous passion in others to defend her interests, and she was not above using it. For instance, in support of her request to Governor Mario Cuomo of New York for the release of three AIDS sufferers in Sing Sing prison (she called these victims the *Lepers of the West*), she added the leverage of her friend Mayor Ed Koch, who announced that he felt like "a blessed instrument to be the vehicle for making this request." He could not believe that anyone would say no to Mother Teresa (Spink 1997).

THE MORAL FRAME

The moral frame is my own contribution to situational leadership theory. In my view, the moral frame completes situational leadership theory. Without it, leaders could just as easily use their leadership skills for promoting evil as for promoting good. Leaders operating out of the moral frame are concerned about their obligations and responsibilities to their followers. Moral frame leaders use some type of moral compass to direct their behavior. They practice what has been described as servant leadership and are concerned with those individuals and groups that are marginalized in their organizations and in society. In short, they are concerned about equality, fairness, and social justice.

Regarding whether Mother Teresa developed a moral frame lens through which she filtered her leadership behavior; suffice it to point out that she was made a saint by the Roman Catholic Church in 2016.

KEY IDEAS

In many ways, Mother Teresa could be considered the prototype for situational leadership behavior. She appropriately balanced her leadership behavior both across and within the five leadership frames. Like her ideological mentor, Mahatma Gandhi, Mother Teresa was a situational leader who was able to move across and within the five leadership frames. One of her colleagues during her Calcutta days recalled Mother Teresa's use of the human resource frame, for which she is best known, but also of the structural, symbolic, political, and of course moral frames when it was appropriate.

> I witnessed not only the love and luminous smile for which she became increasingly internationally renowned but also her practical abilities, the way in which she liked to rearrange the furniture in the sisters' houses, the efficiency which meant that somehow everything was perfectly organized and administered without any organization or administration, the lack of sentimentality

and the immense shrewdness that went hand in hand with intuitive understanding, the earthly qualities which did not detract from her spirituality but which were somehow molded by it. I came to know her humor and her toughness. She was, I discovered, not only humble and small but also strong-willed, resolute, determined and totally fearless, because God was on her side. (Spink 1997, vii)

There is much to gain in emulating the leadership enactments that Mother Teresa modeled for us.

Chapter Twelve

Pope Francis I

Truth is like a precious stone. Offer it in your hand, and it draws others to you; hurl it at someone, and it causes injury.
—*Pope Francis I*

Pope Francis I was born in 1936 in Buenos Aires, Argentina. He worked for a few years before entering the seminary to become a Roman Catholic priest. He was ordained in 1969 and from 1973 to 1979 served as the Jesuit provincial for Argentina. He became bishop of Buenos Aires in 1998 and was ordained a cardinal in 2001. He led the Argentine church during some very turbulent times, but his reputation and popularity withstood the country's "dirty war" in which over ten thousand Argentines disappeared in anticommunist witch hunts and the country's more recent right-wing dictatorships.

Following the resignation of Pope Benedict XVI in 2013, Francis was elected Pope. He chose Francis as his papal name in honor of Saint Francis of Assisi, who was noted for the same characteristics that Francis has displayed. Francis is the first Jesuit pope, the first from the Americas, and the first non-European pope since Pope Gregory III in 741, who was born in Syria.

Throughout his life, Pope Francis has been recognized for his humility; concern for the needy, especially the poor; and his commitment to ecumenism. These characteristics are evident in the way he has conducted himself as a pope. For example, he chose to reside in the Domus Sanctae Marthae guesthouse instead of the Apostolic Palace that was used by his recent predecessors. In addition, he is known for favoring simpler vestments devoid of excessive ornamentation. In another demonstration of humility, he kept the same pectoral cross that he had as a cardinal.

Pope Francis's positions that the Church should be more open, welcoming, and merciful are well known. He is against unregulated capitalism and consumerism, but is also against Marxist communism. He maintains traditional Catholic social teaching regarding abortion, birth control, and homosexuality, and he is against the ordination of women and in favor of celibacy. As an activist pope, Francis is credited with having helped bring about the restoration of diplomatic relations between the United States and Cuba (Ivereigh 2014).

SITUATIONAL LEADERSHIP ANALYSIS

Situational models of leadership differ from earlier trait and behavioral models in asserting that no single way of leading works in all situations. Rather, appropriate behavior depends on the circumstances at a given time. Effective managers diagnose the situation, identify the leadership style or behavior that will be most effective, and then determine whether they can implement the required style.

As we shall see, Francis seems very comfortable with adjusting his leadership style to the situation. His biographers describe him as being decisive, but also discerning and collaborative. He has been critical of himself when he failed to be collaborative enough. "I did not always do the necessary consultation," he said. "My authoritarian and quick manner of making decisions led me to have serious problems" (Ivereigh 2014, 190).

Francis was a disciple of Romano Guardini, a German priest-philosopher who believed in the principles of situational leadership theory and the need for an effective leader to alternate between placing authority outside oneself and in another human being or institution, and placing authority in oneself but ultimately recognizing God as the authority for human life, setting each human being free to become a whole person.

Francis also dealt with the Charismatic movement in the Catholic Church in a flexible and situational way. At first, Francis was suspicious of the emotionality of the Charismatic movement. But when the situation changed—he got to know the movement and its disciples better—he was converted. The conversion materialized in 1999, when he began celebrating an annual Mass for the movement's followers in Buenos Aires.

THE STRUCTURAL FRAME

Structural frame leaders seek to develop a new model of the relationship of structure, strategy, and environment for their organizations. Strategic planning, extensive preparation, and effecting change are priorities for them. As a member of the pro-Peron group in the 1970s, Francis developed the structural and political frame tactic that would be at the foundation of his leadership behavior for the rest of this life—avoiding direct confrontation, while gradually weakening the opposition's resistance in indirect ways, then moving suddenly when least expected.

Francis had the structural frame habit of clearly outlining his goals at the outset of every leadership position that he held. For example, in speaking to journalists on a flight back from Rio de Janeiro, in his first year as pope, Francis would acclaim one of the primary themes of his papacy—a message of mercy. Combining symbolic with structural frame behavior, he recalled how, in the Gospel, rather than call him to account for the money he had squandered, the Prodigal Son's father instead threw a party. "He didn't just wait for him; he was proactive [structural frame] and went out to meet him. That's mercy," Francis said (Ivereigh 2014, 12).

When appropriate, Francis readily engaged in structural frame leadership. For example, in cases when a seminarian was having a vocation crisis where he had doubts about whether he was suited for the celibacy requirement of the priesthood, Francis often suggested that the seminarian leave the seminary. "I help him to leave in peace so he can be a good Christian and not a bad priest" (Ivereigh 2014, 48).

Likewise, as a young teacher in the Jesuit formation program, Francis was known for using structural frame behavior, but always with a dose of human resource frame behavior. His students described him as one who handed out harsh punishments but with an "angelic face." In one instance, he allowed a recalcitrant student's classmates to mete out the discipline. When the student arrived in Francis's office to ascertain his punishment, he was met with a circle of his classmates who acted as sort of a kangaroo court and decided on his punishment. The student in question was suspended from sports for two weeks (Ivereigh 2014).

Francis used structural frame behavior in the form of homilies that gently but firmly made his points. In one such homily, he criticized what he called "spiritual worldliness." According to Francis, this is a disease with many symptoms: "high-spending prelates, airport bishops who often were absent from their dioceses, bishops who flitted from one gala dinner to another, Catholic businessmen and women who stretched the code of ethics to advance their business interests, dioceses that idolized efficiency and put plans before people, self-appointed inquisitors who combed priests' homilies in search of heterodoxy and church organizations that were so professional that they were indistinguishable from those of the secular world" (Ivereigh 2014, 86).

Francis used structural frame enactments to further refine his position and aims regarding spiritual worldliness. The four major areas of spiritual worldliness on which he would focus would be (1) the poor, (2) politics, (3) education, and (4) dialogue with other churches and faiths. In that light, he increased the number of slum priests, established several new Catholic schools, called for a pathway to citizenship for undocumented migrants, and reached out to leaders of other faiths.

Francis utilized structural frame behavior when as a provincial he clearly and publicly outlined his strategic plan: encouraging personal integrity and consolidating people and property, redeploying Jesuits to the periphery, and encouraging vocations while renewing formation. Then he used some symbolic frame behavior and labeled the movement "History and Change." Likewise, during the so-called "dirty war," Francis widely promulgated his two primary objectives: (1) protect the Jesuits and (2) assist the victims of repression.

Because of Francis's facility with the structural frame, Father Pedro Arrupe, the famous Jesuit worldwide provincial during the 1970s and 1980s, enlisted him to head off an internecine plan of the Spanish Jesuits to form a mini-province that would report directly to the pope. Pope Paul VI rejected their request, but the so-called "Jesuits of Fidelity" movement persisted under the leadership of an Argentinean Jesuit. Since this priest was in Francis's province, he had jurisdiction over him. Having very little patience with radicals of any sort, Francis ordered the priest under pain of obedience to leave Rome and return to Argentina immediately—so much for the Jesuits of Fidelity movement!

In the face of the international priest sex abuse scandal, Francis engaged in structural frame behavior and appointed a commission to advise him on reviewing church policies and specifically the pastoral care of sexual abuse victims. Its members included Cardinal Sean O'Malley of Boston, the US bishop who had in his own archdiocese led a radical reform of the Church's handling of these issues, as well as a sexual-abuse victim and an Irish civil rights activist, Marie Collins. "We must proceed with zero tolerance," he instructed the committee (Ivereigh 2014, 128).

As director of Jesuit formation, Francis used structural frame behavior in developing a three-point strategy. The first point was a revision of the study program, separating out philosophy and theology and initiating a two-year arts and humanity requirement. The second element was a pastoral outreach among the local population that included service to the poor. The third prong of the formation reform was the deepening of the postulants' Ignatian spirituality, especially Ignatian discernment.

In another example of the use of structural frame enactments, Francis eventually developed the internalized four principles that undergirded everything that he did. The first, unity comes before conflict; second, the whole comes before the part; third, time comes before conflict; and fourth, reality comes before idea. These four principles, declared Francis, "are the axis around which reconciliation can revolve" (Ivereigh 2014, 143).

In an even more dramatic use of structural frame leadership behavior, Francis bravely challenged the mafias who ruled the Buenos Aires underworld of gambling, people trafficking, prostitution, and child and sweatshop labor. He publically supported a strike of casino workers against their mafia overlords and instructed his pastors to speak out from the pulpit with their condemnation of the mafia's criminal activity.

In one final example of Francis's use of structural frame activity, less than a month after his election as pope, he created an unprecedented council of eight cardinals from across the world to advise him in the governance of the universal Church and to plan the much-needed reform of the Roman Curia. He described the "C8" as "the beginning of a Church with an organization that is not just top-down but also horizontal" (Ivereigh 2014, 372).

THE HUMAN RESOURCE FRAME

Human resource leaders believe in people and communicate that belief. They are passionate about productivity through people. Having seen Francis up close and personal on at least two occasions when he visited Philadelphia in 2015, I can attest firsthand to his effective use of the human resource frame. His magnetic personality and obvious concern for people literally draw people of all ages to him.

Stories of Francis's use of the human resource frame abound. For example, as he began to make the rounds of the Vatican, he encountered a Swiss Guard standing outside his door and brought him a chair. "But Holy Father, I cannot sit down. My boss does not allow it," the guard exclaimed. "Well, I'm the boss of your boss, and I say it's fine," declared Francis (Ivereigh 2014, 85).

Francis demonstrated his penchant for using human resource frame leadership behavior, albeit supplemented by symbolic frame behavior, when soon after his election as pope and upon learning that upward of twenty-five thousand North African refugees lost their lives trying to cross the sea to Italy, he made Lampedusa, 180 miles off the coast of Africa, the site of his first papal visit (Ivereigh 2014)

Although Francis never voted in a political election, once he became a priest he had a natural affinity with the cultural and political tradition represented by Peronism (political philosophy of Argentinean president Juan Peron). As such, he manifested his human resource frame leanings by becoming a member of the local Catholic Action Club in his parish. He was attracted to both Catholic Action and Peronism as a true reflection of the values of ordinary people and as a means of addressing their needs.

Francis's thinking in regard to the importance of the human resource frame was influenced by St. Alberto Hurtado, a Chilean Jesuit who was a pioneering priest in the pursuit of social justice. To Father Hurtado, poverty was a scandal that flew in the face of Chile's claim to be a Catholic, Christian country, and he famously held that charity should only begin where justice ends. It was this model of championing the rights of the underserved that Francis sought to imitate.

Accordingly, Francis believed that "The worst that can happen to a human being is to allow oneself to be swept along by the light of reason. . . . Our mission is instead to discover the seeds of the Word within *humanity*," he declared. The Jesuit Society is "opposed to the homogenizing internationalist which, either by reason or by force, denies peoples their right to be themselves" (Ivereigh 2014, 64).

In another display of human resource frame behavior, when Francis first became a bishop, he would forgo the use of the official limousine and chauffeur, preferring to drive himself. But in so doing, he made certain that he found another job for his driver. Likewise, the attendance at his first homilies as pope was typical in that boisterous crowds assembled in St. Peter's Square. But what was atypical was that there were very few in attendance from his Argentinean homeland. That was because Francis had stopped a campaign to raise funds for pilgrims to travel to Rome, instructing the organizers to distribute the money they had collected to the poor instead (Ivereigh 2014).

THE SYMBOLIC FRAME

In the symbolic frame, the organization is seen as a stage, a theater in which every actor plays certain roles, and the symbolic frame leader attempts to communicate the right impressions to the right audiences. As with virtually all the leaders profiled here, Pope Francis is very active in the symbolic frame.

Francis used symbolic frame leadership behavior in one of his first homilies as Pope. He celebrated an outdoor Mass at one of Rome's largest sports facilities and his homily was on forgiveness and on the need to "care for the person (*cura personalis*)." During the talk, Francis took God's famous question to Cain in Genesis—"Where is your brother?"—and asked, "Who is responsible for this blood?" He then alluded to the parable of the Good Samaritan, likening "us"—he included himself—to the Levite and the priest who passes by: "We are often like the priest and feel sorry for the poor soul, but ultimately engage in 'the culture of comfort' and pass the victim by." Of course, Francis urged us to be more like the Levite (Ivereigh 2014, 2).

Francis again used the symbolic frame in his first year as Pope when he spoke before a group of jobless mine workers on his papal visit to Sardinia. There he told them that he knew what it was like to suffer from financial crisis because his parents lived through the Great Depression and had often spoke of it. He had learned that "where there is no work, there is no dignity," adding that it was an "economic system that brings about such a tragedy; an economic system that has at its center an idol which is called money" (Ivereigh 2014, 3).

Ever conscious of the effect of symbolic frame leadership behavior, even in others, then Cardinal Bergoglio (Francis I) told his friend Rabbi Abraham Skorka that the use of the slogan "Cristo Vence" (Christ Conquers) by then president Juan Peron as a justification for killing hundreds of union demonstrators disgusted him because Peron was using the name of Christ for purely political purposes. In effect, Francis was accusing Peron of using religion to justify the cold-blooded murder of innocent people.

Pope Francis often used symbolic frame behavior in the form of humor to disarm his critics. After he made a searing critique of trickle-down economics in his first major document as pope, he was accused of being a Marxist by some conservatives in the United States. "Marxist ideology is wrong," he told a journalist, but "I have met many Marxists in my life who are good people, so I don't feel offended" (Ivereigh 2014, 37). Francis again used symbolic frame behavior in the form of humor when a woman in Buenos Aires complained to him that her son was in his thirties and still had not gotten married. Francis said to the woman, "Stop ironing his shirts."

Francis liked to put human nature's dilemmas in symbolic terms. For example, he coined a slogan, "Laboratory versus Frontier," to describe the dilemma that Jesuit priests in South America often encountered when deciding to have the people come to them or to go out to the people. Francis would challenge his fellow Jesuits not to be satisfied with mediocrity and wait for the people to come to them for their "words of wisdom" (the Laboratory); instead, he encouraged them to immerse themselves among the people (the Frontier).

In a similar vein, Francis used symbolism to explain the enduring of pain as a means to salvation. According to Francis, in enduring our pain we are imitating the crucified Christ and what was once pointless becomes redemptive—the Catholic and Christian tradition of "offering it up" in the face of pain.

Francis even used symbolic frame leadership behavior in choosing his papal name. He took the name Francis in honor of St. Francis of Assisi, the iconic figure who in the eyes of most Catholics conjures up the image of a humble, poor, and simple man who is the antithesis of the institutional church. After keeping his old black shoes, carrying his own bags, refusing the papal limousine, and keeping his old silver pectoral cross (the pope's is usually gold) just as a start, he joked with the cardinals by saying, "May God forgive you for what you have done [in electing him Pope]" (Ivereigh 2014, 83).

In another symbolic gesture, Francis coined the term "pueblo fiel" (the faithful people) as a concept through which he would filter his leadership enactments. He did not believe that the clergy or the bishops of Rome were in possession of the "truth" that they distributed downward, but instead that the Holy Spirit was revealed through a dialogue among the "pueblo fiel."

Always conscious of the power of symbolism, in his very first months as Pope, Francis met with six clerical abuse survivors in individual meetings at the Vatican. Some leaders of abuse victims' groups described the event as a pure public-relations ploy, but one survivor, Marie Kane, said: "There was a lot of empathy. There was no looking at watches. I was the one who ended it as I had said all I wanted to say." Francis later begged for the victims' forgiveness. "Before God and his people I express my sorrow for the sins and grave crime of clerical sexual abuse committed against you. And I humbly ask forgiveness," he said (Ivereigh 2014, 129). And on the equally controversial subject of gay people in the Church, Francis made the world sit up and take notice with another display of symbolic frame leadership behavior. "Who am I to judge this person?" he exclaimed.

In a similar display of symbolic behavior, Francis was determined to recast the Church as "tender mother" rather than "harsh judge." He believes that the Church's primary task is in healing wounds. He then used a surprising image or symbol to reinforce his point. "I see the Church as a field hospital after battle. It is useless to ask a seriously injured person if he has high cholesterol and about the level of his blood sugars! You have to heal the wounds" (Ivereigh 2014, 169).

On the other hand, one can use symbolism to an extreme (style over substance), and Francis often spoke out against its misuse. "Triumphalism," wrote Francis, "is a way of avoiding the Cross through attachment to progress (or the appearance of it), the technification of the Spirit, the 'Coca-Cola-ization of religious life." According to Francis, spiritual worldliness was putting oneself at the center. It was what Jesus saw the Pharisees doing, when they gave glory to themselves (Ivereigh 2014, 207).

Francis's first papal encyclical is filled with symbolism. In *Evangelii Gaudium*, Francis believed that his encyclical was most powerful when it captured his vision of what he symbolically called the "Samaritan Church," the Church that heals by direct *personal* contact. But the part of the encyclical that attracted most media attention was Francis's critique of the free market's trickle-down theories that trusted the market to set wages and working conditions. However, Francis was only harkening back to the sentiment of Leo XIII's over-one-hundred-year-old encyclical *Rerum Novarum* (1891), which also criticized the enrichment of the few at the expense of the many.

Francis was also criticized in some circles by another of his symbolic frame practices. As Pope, in imitation of Christ famously washing the feet of his apostles, Francis symbolically washed the feet at Easter of twelve juvenile detainees, one of whom was a Serbian girl who became the first Muslim and the first woman ever to have her feet washed by a pope. Despite the criticism, Francis continues this symbolic practice every Easter.

For one final example of Pope Francis's frequent use of the symbolic frame, we need only look at his devotion to an obscure figure in the Catholic Church, Mary the Untier of Knots. Whereas most prelates engage in the symbolic gesture of handing out a prayer card of their favorite saint upon meeting someone, Francis also does so, but with a figure who is little known among ordinary Catholics, much less non-Catholics and nonbelievers—a holy card of Mary the Untier of Knots.

Francis became enamored with the symbolism of a little-known German painting known as Maria Knotenloserin, or Mary the Untier of Knots. His devotion grew out of the story of a feuding married couple who had been on the verge of separation and divorce. A family friend who was a Jesuit priest prayed to the Virgin Mary to untie all the knots that were leading the couple to divorce. Peace was ultimately restored and the marriage was saved. Thus began Francis's habit of praying to Mary the Untier of Knots to help him resolve his most difficult dilemmas (Ivereigh 2014).

THE POLITICAL FRAME

Leaders operating out of the political frame clarify what they want and what they can get. Political leaders are realists above all. They never let what they want cloud their judgment about what is possible. They assess the distribution of power and interests. They are primarily concerned with "making friends and influencing people." It took awhile, but Francis developed and fine-tuned his ability to engage in political frame leadership behavior over the years. Call it what you will, charisma, charm, but essentially it is the capacity to read people, gain their trust, and convince them to forgo their self-interest in the pursuit of the common good. In short, it is the ability to convince oneself and others of the value of compromise.

In this light, Francis's favorite Church document was Pope Paul's encyclical, *Evangelii Nuntiandi*, whose great purpose was to *reconcile* eternal Church teachings with the diversity of cultures. And, to a large extent, the ability to do so seems to be one of Francis's greatest strengths.

Perhaps Francis's most prolific use of political frame leadership behavior was during the so-called "dirty war" when he was a prelate in Argentina. It was then that he engaged in the high-wire act of both protecting the lives of his fellow Jesuits and at the same time assisting the victims of the repression. While mollifying the military government with the astute application of political frame behavior, Francis was able to pull it off. During the dirty war (1969–1979), not one Jesuit lost his life, while Francis was able to save the lives of dozens of political refugees. He accomplished this magical feat by not speaking out publicly against the military regime, but instead negotiating behind closed doors.

During this ten-year cycle of violence where a military dictatorship dominated Argentinian politics and an opposing guerrilla group fought for power, Francis was somehow able to befriend both sides, the deposed Peronists and the military junta in the person of the navy chief, Admiral Emilio Massera. He also made good use of the Jesuit military chaplains and both the progressive and moderate bishops. In time, Francis earned the nickname of "La Gioconda," the title of Leonardo Da Vinci's painting of the Mona Lisa, with her famously inscrutable expression (Ivereigh 2014, 137).

In another instance of Francis's effective use of political frame behavior, he publicly supported ten Jesuit priests who had gone on a hunger strike to protest the building of a road that would have claimed substantial property in a slum neighborhood of Buenos Aires. At the same time, he negotiated a behind-the-scenes deal whereby the priests would end their hunger strike and the road would circumvent the slum.

Once again displaying his political frame proclivities, Francis publicly decried the recent tendency of cities and countries to accept same-sex marriage, but made certain to lend his support to revising and extending the benefits to those homosexuals engaged in civil unions. He rarely opposed something without offering a viable alternative—the true mark of a political frame leader (Ivereigh 2014).

THE MORAL FRAME

The moral frame is my own contribution to situational leadership theory. In my view, the moral frame completes situational leadership theory. Without it, leaders could just as easily use their leadership skills for promoting evil as for promoting good. Leaders operating out of the moral frame are concerned about their obligations and responsibilities to their followers. Moral frame leaders use some type of moral compass to direct their behavior. They practice what has been described as servant leadership and are concerned with those individuals and groups that are marginalized in their organizations and in society. In short, they are concerned about equality, fairness, and social justice.

While it is evident that, like every Catholic prelate, Pope Francis I is guided by the moral frame of the life and teachings of Jesus Christ; being a Jesuit, he is dedicated to the added moral lens of the Ignatian Vision or tradition. That is why the strong emphasis of his pontificate has been in the service of the poor and the seeking of social justice.

KEY IDEAS

As we have seen, whether consciously or unconsciously, Pope Francis I is quite comfortable using the principles of situational leadership theory. As a result of his effective use of a variety of leadership frames in different situations, his followers throughout his career have loved him for his simplicity, his directness, his humility, his passion for social justice, and his demonstrative love for children, the elderly, and the disabled. They praise his clear and precise three-point speeches and homilies, his timely references, and his vivid metaphors. They admire his humor and his candor. Francis serves as a truly exemplary role model for leaders and aspiring leaders in any country and in any culture.

Chapter Thirteen

What Have You Learned?

> *The greatest discovery of my generation is that man can alter his life simply by altering his attitude of mind.*
>
> —William James

After each weekly cabinet meeting, a university president I served with would end by going around the table eliciting a one-sentence response to the question: "What have you learned today?" There was a method behind this apparent madness in that knowing that this question would be asked, we paid rapt attention to what was transpiring at the meeting. In this light, I echo that president's question here. What did we learn about leadership from the ten spiritual and religious leaders from all over the world profiled in this study, and is it applicable to every nation and culture?

First, we learned that situational leadership theory makes common sense. Virtually all these leaders were effective because they were able to adapt their leadership behavior to changing situations. None of them was "stuck" in one paradigm. Some might be criticized for using one or another leadership frame too exclusively, but the reality is that, by and large, they were successful because, to a person, they were able to very effectively balance their use of the four leadership frames enunciated by Lee Bolman and Terrence Deal. And, being spiritual and religious leaders, they all developed a moral frame through which they could critically examine their leadership behavior.

More specifically, we have learned that there are four requisites for effective leadership no matter one's society or culture:

1. a *knowledge* of, and *passion* for, one's field (job competency).
2. an ability to engender mutual *trust and respect* with one's followers (moral frame behavior).

3. a knowledge of the organizational and societal *culture* (readiness level) of one's followers.
4. an ability to apply *situational leadership theory* to one's practice.

LEADERSHIP BEHAVIORS

Lest one be confused about what leadership behaviors fit into what frames, here are some examples:

Structural Frame Behaviors

- developing a vision
- setting goals
- developing a strategic plan
- implementing the plan
- proposing and implementing change in the form of improvements
- closely supervising followers
- developing rules and regulations
- developing job descriptions and responsibilities
- striving for the magis (continuous improvement)
- demonstrating competency (knowledgeable, organized, industrious, passionate, committed)
- hands-on managing
- attending to detail
- lifelong learning
- meticulously preparation
- behaving authoritatively
- using analytical and logical thinking
- mastering the technical aspects of one's profession

Human Resource Frame Behaviors

- developing a system of rewards to motivate employees
- giving praise for accomplishments
- empowering others
- concern for the individual (*cura personalis*)
- participative decision making
- team building
- acknowledging special occasions (e.g., birthdays, anniversaries, get-well sentiments)
- managing by walking around (being visible)

Symbolic Frame Behaviors

- concern for one's personal appearance
- modeling desired behavior
- motivational speeches and publications
- inspirational quotes, slogans, adages, etc. (on letterhead/posters)
- displaying symbols of achievement in the workplace
- telling stories, jokes, etc.
- being visible

Political Frame Behaviors

- negotiating a contract or covenant on compensation and working conditions
- lobbying for improvements
- fund raising and institutional development activities
- making compromises (quid pro quo)
- building political and social capital
- engaging in a Force Field Analysis (neutralizing opposing forces) to effect change

Moral Frame Behaviors

- developing a personal moral compass to guide one's behavior
- striving for the magis (the greater good)
- modeling personal integrity and moral character (being honest and forthright)
- being sensitive to the human needs of all (*cura personalis*), especially the marginalized in the workplace
- being concerned about equality, fairness, and social justice in the workplace and in society

GLOBAL LEADERSHIP IMPLICATIONS

By and large, we learned that although all cultures have their unique idiosyncrasies, Bolman and Deal's situational leadership model, by its very nature (situational), seems to work within and across cultures. Basically, we saw that what worked for Jesus Christ, Moses, Mohammad, Gandhi, and Mother Teresa in the Mideast worked for Buddha and Confucius in the East and Martin Luther King, Pope St. Paul II, and Pope Francis in the West—our conclusion being that from a global perspective, the basic tenets of situational leadership theory seem to transcend all cultures and nations. So our study confirmed the outcome of both Caroline Rook and Anupam Agrawal's study *Global Leaders East and West—Do All Global Leaders Lead in the Same*

Way? and Robert J. House's study *How Cultural Factors Affect Leadership* (Rook and Agrawal 2013; House 1999).

In their working paper, Rook and Agrawal suggest that Eastern and Western management styles could be likened to pieces of music that use basically the same notes but sometimes the patterns might vary. Utilizing Manfed Kets de Vries's Global Executive Leadership Inventory, Rook and Agrawal analyzed data from 1,748 middle- and top-level executives representing 128 nationalities and found that even with all the nuances among different cultures, any competent leader could rather readily adapt his or her leadership behavior or enactments to the vagaries of the global environment.

Robert J. House reached similar conclusions back in 1999. House used his Global Leadership and Organizational Behavior Effectiveness Research Program to test leadership hypotheses in various world cultures. He found that although there are culturally contingent leadership attributes that help or hinder leadership, for the most part there are many universally endorsed leadership attributes that transcend culture and geographic location. It all comes down to the leader's ability to effectively adapt his or her behavior to the environment or culture in which she or he functions—the fundamental tenet of situational leadership theory.

TEACHERS AS LEADERS

When we think of educational leaders, we most often think in terms of administrators. While this is natural, we would argue that the classroom teacher is as much a leader in his or her own way as a principal, a superintendent, or a college president. Certainly, every classroom teacher assumes the role of instructional leader and if given responsibility for chairing a curriculum committee or directing an extracurricular activity, also serves as a leader in those roles. So to some extent, we all serve a leadership role in one form or another in some aspect of our personal and/or professional lives. Thus, what we have learned from the leaders profiled in this book should be applicable and helpful to all of us to one extent or another.

We believe that the principles of situational leadership theory are constant and apply to all of us in our differing leadership roles. Using Bolman and Deal's situational leadership model, for example, one can easily envision classroom teachers exhibiting structural frame leadership behavior in improving their classroom effectiveness by furthering their education, or by enforcing a strict code of conduct in their classrooms to create an atmosphere more conducive to learning. Those same teachers would do well to temper their leadership behavior with a modicum of human resource frame behavior by treating their students with the proverbial "velvet glove" when appropriate.

To complete their use of situational leadership theory, the teacher-leader could engage in symbolic frame behavior in the form of acting and dressing in a professional manner and by "showing the flag" in attending some of the schools' extracurricular activities. Political frame leadership behavior can be practiced by volunteering to direct the Sunshine Fund, getting involved in the school's fundraisers, or perhaps running for union representative. Finally, the moral frame can be operationalized by treating all of the students with equanimity and having the same academic expectations of all of them, no matter their race, creed, ability level, class, or gender.

To be an effective situational teacher-leader, therefore, the classroom teacher needs to be introspective with regard to his or her role as an instructional leader. In other words, we have to think hard about what we say and do in the presence of our students and colleagues. The well-known psychiatrist and educational philosopher Dr. William Glasser suggests that in developing our daily lesson plans, for example, we consciously incorporate at least one or two activities that would address each of the four frames of leadership enunciated by Bolman and Deal.

Thus, attending to details like taking roll every day and strictly enforcing a classroom discipline code may be a way to cover the structural frame. Being sensitive to and addressing the needs of our special students in a creative way might be a way to satisfy the human resource frame. While varying one's teaching style to the learning styles of the students by occasionally showing a video or making a Power Point presentation or engaging the students in some type of learning game (spelling bee) or cooperative learning activity would be an example of incorporating the symbolic frame into one's lesson plans. Finally, offering the students an occasional quid pro quo in the form of no homework for good behavior may be a way of incorporating political frame behavior into the classroom.

Another consideration for teacher-leaders is Hersey and Blanchard's idea of readiness (chapter 1). We are all familiar with Piaget's stages of development and the need to be aware of the instructional readiness level of our students, but we may be less aware of our need to accurately gauge our students' readiness for accepting our leadership behavior. As we have seen, Hersey and Blanchard's rule of thumb is to utilize structural frame or directing behavior with students who are at a low readiness level, while employing human resource, symbolic and political frame leadership behavior or coaching and delegating behavior as the student's readiness level moves higher. Of course, we have to also be careful to distinguish between individual readiness and group (the entire class) readiness, each of which may be at different levels. Finally, in our application of these leadership principles, we should remember the slogan: *Everything in moderation, except moderation.*

THE IMPORTANCE OF THEORY

We cannot underestimate the value and importance of theory in the field of leadership, and in any other field for that matter. As indicated earlier in this chapter, in the fourth requisite for effective leadership, without theory we have no valid way of diagnosing, analyzing, and correcting failed practice. Without a theoretical base, we oftentimes lead by trial and error, or by the proverbial "seat of your pants."

Theory is to leadership as the fundamentals are to athletics. For example, if a basketball player is suddenly shooting a lower percentage than his or her career average, something is obviously wrong. He or she has experienced "failed practice." What to do? Most athletes in this situation are coached to "go back to the basics or the fundamentals." The basketball player will review the fundamentals of shooting, like squaring oneself to the basket, keeping the shooting elbow in, keeping the guide-hand off the ball upon release, snapping the wrist and exaggerating one's follow-through. It is likely that one or more of these fundamentals is being violated and causing the shooting percentage decline and when corrected, the percentage will rise again to its most recent average.

If the athlete does not know the fundamentals of shooting, *shooting theory* if you will, he or she can only correct the problem through the very inefficient means of trial and error. The same goes for leaders who are losing their impact on their followers. If they have not adopted a leadership theory to guide their leadership behavior, they can only correct the leadership decline by trial and error.

However, if the leader has adopted a leadership theory, the leader can review the tenets or principles of the theory and most likely diagnose the deficiency and correct it rather quickly. For example, the leader might find that his or her followers are no longer responding to the leader's friendly persuasion and active support (human resource frame leadership behavior). In analyzing the *situation*, and the evolving readiness level of the followers, the leader might conclude that he or she is using human resource frame behavior with the followers when structural frame leadership behavior may be more appropriate. As a result of this analysis, the leader may decide to utilize a more structural frame approach and "lay down the law" to his or her recalcitrant followers. This rather simple example demonstrates the importance and value of theory in providing leaders with a method or pedagogy to be able to diagnose and correct failed practice in an efficient and effective way.

LEADING WITH MIND

Knowledge of one's field is a sine qua non for effective leadership. This quality usually manifests itself in one's structural frame leadership behavior. In sports terms, the leader must have a good command of the fundamentals and strategies of the game. In business terms, the effective leader must have a thorough knowledge of the technical aspects of how a business operates and a sense of how to develop a viable business plan. In education, the leader needs to know how schools and school systems operate and what the best practices in the field are in curriculum and instruction.

In a family situation, the leader (parent or guardian) needs to have at least a modicum of knowledge regarding the principles of child psychology. In short, leaders in any field need to know that field and be able to apply that knowledge through the theory and practice of organizational development which would include the following:

a. Organizational Structure: how an institution is organized.
b. Organizational Culture: the values and beliefs of an institution.
c. Motivation: the system of rewards and incentives provided.
d. Communication: the clarity and accuracy of the communication process.
e. Decision Making: how and by whom decisions are made.
f. Conflict Management: how dysfunctional conflict is handled.
g. Power Distribution: how the power in an institution is distributed.
h. Strategic Planning: how the mission, vision, and strategic plan are developed.
i. Change: how change is effectively implemented in an institution.

We will not go into detail about these processes here. If the reader is interested in a comprehensive look at these processes, I would recommend my book, *A Ten-Minute Approach to Educational Leadership*. However, included at the end of this chapter is a pair of diagnostic tools entitled "The Heart Smart Survey I and II," which I developed to help leaders assess the organizational health of their institutions and to identify which of the factors listed above are in need of improvement.

LEADING WITH HEART

To recap, then, the effective leader needs to be *technically* competent. However, being technically competent is not enough. To be truly effective and heroic, leaders also need to master the *art* of leadership and learn to lead with *heart*. In effect, leaders need to operate out of both the structural and political frames (science) and the human resources, symbolic, and moral frames (art) to maximize their effectiveness. This means that they must be concerned about the person (*cura personalis*). They must abide by the Golden Rule and treat others as they wish to be treated.

As noted in chapter 2, truly effective leaders treat their employees like volunteers and empower them to actualize their true potential, thus engendering mutual trust and respect among virtually all of their workplace colleagues.

In their book entitled *Leading with Kindness* (2008), William Baker and Michael O'Malley reiterate my views. They explore how one of the most unheralded features of leadership, basic human kindness, drives successful organizations. And while most scholars generally recognize that a leader's emotional intelligence factors into that person's leadership behavior, most are reticent to consider it to be as important as analytical ability, decision-making skills, or implementation skills. Such emotions as compassion, empathy, and kindness are often dismissed as unquantifiable, and are often seen as weaknesses. Yet, research in neuroscience and the social sciences clearly reveals that one's physiological and emotional states have measurable effects on both individual and group performance. In an earlier work, *Feminist Theory and Leadership*, we have found that women leaders are particularly adept at effectively utilizing their emotional intelligence in the form of showing human kindness. Perhaps we should all follow their lead.

In the jargon of the day, individuals who lead with heart or kindness are said to have a high degree of emotional intelligence. Most of us are familiar with the current notion of multiple intelligences; that is, individuals have a number of intelligences in addition to cognitive intelligence. Among these intelligences is emotional intelligence. Several theories within the emotional intelligence paradigm seek to understand how individuals perceive, understand, utilize, and manage emotions in an effort to predict and foster personal effectiveness.

Most of these models define emotional intelligence as an array of traits and abilities related to emotional and social knowledge that influence our overall ability to effectively cope with environmental demands; as such, emotional intelligence can be viewed as a model of psychological well-being and adaptation. This includes the ability to be aware of, to understand, and to relate to others; the ability to deal with strong emotions and to control one's impulses; and the ability to adapt to change and to solve problems of a personal and social nature. The five main domains of these models are intrapersonal skills, interpersonal skills, adaptability, stress management, and general mood. If the reader sees a similarity between emotional intelligence and what we call *leading with heart* and what Baker and O'Malley call *leading with kindness*, it is not coincidental.

LEADING WITH MIND AND HEART

So, the truly heroic leaders lead with *both* mind (science) and heart (art)—with cognitive intelligence and emotional intelligence. One or the other will not suffice. Only by mastering both will the leader succeed. For example, one could argue that former president William Clinton was rendered ineffective as a leader because of the Monica Lewinsky affair and was nearly impeached. Why? Because he suddenly lost the *knowledge* of how government works (science)? No! He lost his ability to lead because he lost the *trust and respect* of much of the American public (art). He could still lead with his mind, but he had lost the ability to lead with heart. It is only recently, several years later, that he is reestablishing his integrity with the American public.

To the contrary, one could argue that former president Jimmy Carter lost his ability to lead because of a perceived lack of competency. Right or wrong, the majority of the voting public did not believe that he had the knowledge necessary to manage government operations and effectively lead with mind. On the other hand, virtually no one questioned his concern for people, his integrity, and his ability to lead with heart. Absent the perceived ability to do *both*, however, he lost the 1980 election to Ronald Reagan.

We conclude, then, that effective leaders are situational; that is, they are capable of adapting their leadership behavior to the situation. They utilize structural, human resources, symbolic political, and moral frame leadership behavior when appropriate. They lead with both mind (structural and political behavior) and with heart (human resources, symbolic, and moral behavior). They master both the science (mind) and art (heart) of leadership, and in doing so, they are transformational, leading their organizations and sometimes their entire societies to new heights. As Chris Lowney (2003) writes in *Heroic Leadership*, such leaders are, in a word, truly "heroic."

ORGANIZATIONAL CULTURE

Effectively balancing the use of the five frames of leadership behavior assumes that the leader has a thorough knowledge and understanding of the leader's organizational culture, and from what we learned in this study, the societal culture. In the words of Harold Hill in *The Music Man*, the leader needs "to know the territory." Knowing the territory, or knowing the organizational and societal culture, means that the leader must know the beliefs, expectations, and shared values of the organization, as well as the personality of the individuals and the organization as a whole. Without such knowledge, the leader cannot appropriately apply the correct leadership frame to the situation.

As mentioned in chapter 1, Paul Hersey and Ken Blanchard contribute to our understanding of what it means to know the culture of the organization and the broader culture with their concept of *readiness level*. They define readiness level as the follower's ability and willingness to accomplish a specific task; this is the major contingency that influences what leadership frame should be applied. Follower readiness incorporates the follower's level of achievement motivation, ability, and willingness to assume responsibility for his or her own behavior in accomplishing specific tasks, as well as his or her education and experience relevant to the task. So, a person with a low readiness level should be dealt with by using structural frame behavior (telling behavior), while a person with a very high readiness level should be dealt with using human resource and symbolic frame behavior (delegating behavior).

At this point, the reader may be thinking that using leadership theory to determine one's leadership behavior is an exercise in futility. How can one be realistically expected to assess accurately and immediately the individual's or group's readiness level before acting? It seems like an utterly complex and overwhelming task. At the risk of being too simplistic, when confronted with this reaction, I often relate using leadership theory to determine one's leadership behavior to riding a bike. When we first learn to ride a bike, we have to concern ourselves with keeping our balance, steering, pedaling, and being ready to brake at a moment's notice. However, once we learn and have had experience riding the bike, we seldom think of those details. We have learned to ride the bike by instinct or habit.

Having used situational leadership theory to determine my own leadership behavior, I can attest to the fact that its use becomes as instinctive as riding a bike after a while. At this point, I can rather consistently assess the readiness level of an individual or group and apply the appropriate leadership frame behavior—and believe me when I say, if I can do it, so can you.

TRANSFORMATIONAL LEADERSHIP

We all aspire to be transformational leaders—leaders who inspire positive change in their followers. As we saw in chapter 1, charismatic or transformational leaders use charisma to inspire their followers. They talk to the followers about how essential their performance is and how they expect the group's performance to exceed expectations. Such leaders use dominance, self-confidence, a need for influence, and conviction of moral righteousness to increase their charisma and consequently their leadership effectiveness. A transformational leader changes an organization by recognizing an opportunity and developing a vision, communicating that vision to organizational members, building trust in the vision, and achieving the vision by motivating organizational members.

Virtually all of the leaders profiled in this book could be considered transformational leaders at some level. In every case, they transformed their cultures in some meaningful and important way. Their effective use of leadership behavior reformed whole societies in many cases. They achieved this success by displaying the characteristics of a situational and transformational leader. They all had a vision and had the personal charisma and ability to convince others to join them in achieving that vision.

In many cases, these spiritual and religious leaders achieved their visions in different ways by applying the appropriate leadership behavior to their differing situations. They were able to gauge the *readiness level* of their followers accurately and apply the appropriate leadership behavior, whether it be structural, human resource, symbolic, political, or moral frame behavior, or some combination thereof. Although this is easier said than done, studying these leaders' leadership behavior as depicted in this book should be helpful to anyone aspiring to become a transformational leader.

LEADERSHIP AS A MORAL SCIENCE

Left on its own, situational leadership theory is secular and amoral. As such, its use is just as likely to produce a leader like Adolf Hitler or, in the more modern era, Slobodan Milosevic, as it is to produce a leader in the mold of the religious and spiritual leaders profiled here.

We have all seen examples of immoral and unethical leadership behavior. Even in education we have witnessed instances of this kind of behavior—examples ranging from the trivial, like stealing a box of paper clips and other school supplies, to the more serious, like fabricating standardized test scores, engaging in multimillion-dollar embezzlements, and stealing to support drug and gambling addictions. So, to ensure that leaders lead with heart as well as mind, we have suggested the use of the Ignatian Vision as a moral lens or hermeneutic through which one views his or her leadership behavior.

As recommended in chapter 2, asking ourselves whether our leadership behavior conforms to Ignatius' principles of the *magis, cura personalis,* discernment, service to others, and social justice will bring to completion our understanding and use of situational leadership theory and transform leadership into a moral science. In my view, using the Ignatian Vision, or one of the moral/ethical codes developed by one or another of the spiritual leaders profiled here as a moral compass to direct our leadership behavior, will help ensure that history will witness more leaders who use their leadership skills to promote good and fewer who use them to promote evil.

AN EFFECTIVE LEADERSHIP FORMULA

For the concrete/sequential thinkers and learners among us, it is oftentimes clearer and more understandable if a complex theory such as situational leadership theory can be placed in mathematical terms. The following is my attempt to do so:

Effective Leadership Behavior = (is a function of)

$$\frac{St + Hr + Pl + Sy \, (Moral)}{Readiness \, Level \, and \, Culture}$$

where St stands for structural frame behavior, Hr stands for human resource frame behavior, Pl stands for political frame behavior, Sy stands for symbolic frame behavior, Moral stands for moral frame behavior, Readiness stands for the maturity (the ability and willingness to perform the task) level of the follower(s), and Culture stands for both the organizational culture and the broader culture which is a function of the unique mores of the society in which one lives.

Thus one would articulate this formula in the following manner: effective leadership behavior is the result of, or the function of, the appropriate application of one or some combination of structural, human resource, political, and symbolic frame behavior, depending on the situation which is made up of the readiness level of the follower(s), the organization's culture and the societal culture in which the leader lives, with the moral frame being a constant.

KEY IDEAS

Recently, a plethora of research studies have been conducted on leadership and leadership styles. The overwhelming evidence indicates that there is not one singular leadership style that is most effective in all situations. Rather, whether one is an American or foreign leader, it has been found that a leader's leadership behavior should be adapted to the situation (organizational and societal culture and readiness level) so that at various times structural, human resource, symbolic, political, or moral frame leadership behavior may be most effective.

The emergence of transformational leadership has seen leadership theory come full circle. Transformational leadership theory combines aspects of early trait theory with the more current situational models. The personal charisma of the leader, along with his or her ability to formulate an organizational vision and communicate it to others while embodying the virtues of trust and respect, determines the transformational leader's effectiveness.

And, based on our observations of the leadership enactments of the religious/spiritual leaders profiled here, the situational nature of leadership seems to transcend the various societies and cultures in which the leader finds him- or herself.

Furthermore, since the effective leader, no matter his or her geographical location or cultural background, is expected to adapt his or her leadership style to an ever-changing environment, leadership becomes an even more complex and challenging task. However, a thorough knowledge of one's local organizational and one's broader societal culture (readiness level of one's followers) and the principles of situational leadership theory can make some sense out of the apparent chaos that a leader often faces on a daily basis. It is my hope that the contents of this book and the effective leadership behavior modeled by the ten great leaders profiled here will shed some light on the *situation*—pun intended.

Diagnostics

THE HEART SMART SURVEY I AND II

Just as there are vital signs in measuring individual health, it is believed that there are vital signs for measuring the health of educational institutions. This survey (Heart Smart Survey I) will help to identify those vital signs in your school or school system. It, along with the Heart Smart Survey II, will indicate further whether the institution's leaders are leading with both mind and heart.

The Heart Smart Survey I

Please think of your present work environment and indicate the degree to which you agree or disagree with each of the following statements. A "1" is Agree Strongly and a "7" is Disagree Strongly.

Agree Strongly	Agree	Agree Slightly	Neither Agree nor Disagree	Disagree Slightly	Disagree	Disagree Strongly
1	2	3	4	5	6	7

1. The manner in which the tasks in this institution are divided is a logical one.
2. The relationships among coworkers are harmonious.
3. This institution's leadership efforts result in its fulfillment of its purposes.
4. My work at this institution offers me an opportunity to grow as a person.
5. I can always talk to someone at work if I have a work-related problem.

6. The faculty actively participates in decisions.
7. There is little evidence of unresolved conflict in this institution.
8. There is a strong fit between this institution's mission and my own values.
9. The faculty and staff are represented on most committees and task forces.
10. Staff development routinely accompanies any significant changes that occur in this institution.
11. The manner in which the tasks in this institution are distributed is a fair one.
12. Older faculty's opinions are valued.
13. The administrators display the behaviors required for effective leadership.
14. The rewards and incentives here are both internal and external.
15. There is open and direct communication among all levels of this institution.
16. Participative decision making is fostered at this institution.
17. What little conflict that exists at this institution is not dysfunctional.
18. Representatives of all segments of the school community participate in the strategic-planning process.
19. The faculty and staff have an appropriate voice in the operation of this institution.
20. This institution is not resistant to constructive change.
21. The division of labor in this organization helps its efforts to reach its goals.
22. I feel valued by this institution.
23. The administration encourages an appropriate amount of participation in decision making.
24. Faculty and staff members are often recognized for special achievements.
25. There are no significant barriers to effective communication at this institution.
26. When the acceptance of a decision is important, a group decision-making model is used.
27. There are mechanisms at this institution to effectively manage conflict and stress.
28. Most of the employees understand the mission and goals of this institution.
29. The faculty and staff feel empowered to make their own decisions regarding their daily work.
30. Tolerance toward change is modeled by the administration of this institution.
31. The various grade level teachers and departments work well together.

32. Differences among people are accepted.
33. The leadership is able to generate continuous improvement in the institution.
34. My ideas are encouraged, recognized, and used.
35. Communication is carried out in a nonaggressive style.
36. In general, the decision-making process is an effective one.
37. Conflicts are usually resolved before they become dysfunctional.
38. For the most part, the employees of this institution feel an "ownership" of its goals.
39. The faculty and staff are encouraged to be creative in their work.
40. When changes are made they do so within a rational process.
41. This institution's organizational design responds well to changes in the internal and external environment.
42. The teaching and the nonteaching staffs get along with one another.
43. The leadership of this institution espouses a clear educational vision.
44. The goals and objectives for the year are mutually developed by the faculty and the administration.
45. I believe that my opinions and ideas are listened to.
46. Usually, a collaborative style of decision making is utilized at this institution.
47. A collaborative approach to conflict resolution is ordinarily used.
48. This institution has a clear educational vision.
49. The faculty and staff can express their opinions without fear of retribution.
50. I feel confident that I will have an opportunity for input if a significant change were to take place in this institution.
51. This institution is "people-oriented."
52. Administrators and faculty have mutual respect for one another.
53. Administrators give people the freedom to do their jobs.
54. The rewards and incentives in this institution are designed to satisfy a variety of individual needs.
55. The opportunity for feedback is always available in the communications process.
56. Group decision-making techniques, like brainstorming and group surveys, are sometimes used in the decision-making process.
57. Conflicts are oftentimes prevented by early intervention.
58. This institution has a strategic plan for the future.
59. Most administrators here use the power of persuasion rather than the power of coercion.
60. This institution is committed to continually improving through the process of change.
61. This institution does not adhere to a strict chain of command.
62. This institution exhibits grace, style, and civility.

63. The administrators model desired behavior.
64. At this institution, employees are not normally coerced into doing things.
65. I have the information that I need to do a good job.
66. I can constructively challenge the decisions in this institution.
67. A process to resolve work-related grievances is available.
68. There is an ongoing planning process at this institution.
69. The faculty and staff have input into the operation of this institution through a collective bargaining unit or through a faculty governance body.
70. The policies, procedures, and programs of this institution are periodically reviewed.

The Heart Smart Survey II

Please think of your present work environment and indicate the degree to which you agree or disagree with each of the following statements. A "1" is Agree Strongly and a "7" is Disagree Strongly.

Agree Strongly	Agree	Agree Slightly	Neither Agree nor Disagree	Disagree Slightly	Disagree	Disagree Strongly
1	2	3	4	5	6	7

1. There is not much evidence of faculty and staff holding and espousing ethical values.
2. There is not much evidence of mutual respect and understanding among the faculty and staff.
3. There is not much of a sense of voluntarism and dedication among the teachers and staff.
4. There is not much indication that teachers and staff have committed themselves to the modeling of moral and ethical values.
5. There is not much trust and respect shared among faculty, staff, and administration.
6. There is little evidence that teachers encourage students to be concerned for the underserved in their communities.
7. There is not much evidence that the teachers are supportive of a moral or ethical code to guide one's behavior.
8. There are not many occasions when the faculty and staff get to interact with one another.
9. There are not many opportunities presented to students to develop an appreciation of and respect for cultures other than their own.
10. Teachers do not often bear witness to their values and beliefs through their daily behavior.

11. The faculty and staff do not seem to support one another in various events and activities.
12. There are not many occasions when faculty members accompany their students on community-service activities.
13. There are no occasions when faculty and students discuss their values and beliefs.
14. There is not much in the way of promotion of justice and fairness among students.
15. There is not a culture that fosters service to the community at this institution.
16. The faculty does not seem to go out of its way to model their belief system to the students.
17. There is not much evidence of the promotion of justice and fairness among teachers.
18. There are not many occasions when teachers engage in community service by donating space, time, resources, and personal help.
19. There are not many times when the faculty and staff articulate or speak out on their values and beliefs.
20. There is not much evidence of the promotion of justice and fairness between teachers and administrators.
21. There are not many instances of faculty evidencing compassion and giving service to the needy, the disadvantaged, and troubled students and coworkers.
22. There are not many occasions when the faculty discusses teaching values and ethics.
23. There are significant barriers to effective communication at this institution.
24. The overall morale of the school is not very good.
25. The faculty and staff do not show much concern for world problems like hunger, poverty, war, pollution, and social justice.
26. The faculty does not openly express its support of ethical and moral values.
27. The conflicts that arise among individuals and groups are not resolved very well.
28. The teachers do not encourage a sense of service and social justice in their students very much.
29. The faculty do not avail themselves of professional-development opportunities to develop their skills in teaching values education.
30. The sense of trust and respect at this institution is not very high.
31. There is a tendency to merely "go through the motions" at this school.
32. There is a tendency for the superficial to be more important than the substantial at this school.

33. There is a dark tension that exists among key individuals at this school.
34. It seems that the attainment of short-term goals is preferred to the achievement of long-term goals.
35. There seems to be a loss of grace, style, and civility at this institution.
36. There is a tendency to do the minimal and not "go the extra yard" at this school.
37. The administration seems to use coercion to motivate employees here.
38. We do not ever seem to be able to find the time to celebrate accomplishments here.
39. The teachers and staff seem to treat students like customers or impositions here.
40. The employees feel manipulated and exploited here.
41. There don't seem to be many stories and storytellers to carry on the tradition at this school.
42. The leaders here seem to want to be served rather than to serve.
43. There seems to be a certain arrogance among the leaders at this school.
44. There seems to be a sense of competition here whereby one person or group's gain always has to be at another's expense.
45. Teachers here won't pick up a piece of paper because "that's the janitor's job."
46. When something goes wrong here, there is a tendency to want to cast blame.
47. Diversity and individual charisma are not respected here.
48. Teachers here seem to use up all their sick days even if they are not sick.
49. The administration seems to accumulate power rather than sharing it at this institution.
50. The climate in this school seems to encourage competition rather than collaboration.
51. Teachers seem to work solely for a paycheck here.
52. Teachers are asked to teach to the test to improve test scores at this school.
53. There is a tendency for the faculty rooms to be sources of malicious gossip and rumors.
54. There is a union mentality here whereby teachers do not want to do anything extra unless they are paid.
55. Administrators here seem to dwell on people's weaknesses rather than their strengths.
56. Individual turf is protected to the detriment of institutional goals at this school.

57. There is definitely a caste system here among the administration, the faculty, and the clerical and custodial staffs.

THE HEART SMART ORGANIZATIONAL DIAGNOSIS

Questionnaires

Just as there are vital signs in measuring individual health, we believe that there are vital signs in measuring the good health of organizations. These surveys will help us to identify those vital signs in your school or school system. The purpose of the Heart Smart Organizational Diagnosis Questionnaires, therefore, is to provide feedback data for intensive diagnostic efforts. Use of the questionnaire, either by itself or in conjunction with other information-collecting techniques such as systematic observation or interviewing, will provide the data needed for identifying strengths and weaknesses in the functioning of an educational institution, and help determine whether the leaders are leading with both mind and heart.

A meaningful diagnostic effort must be based on a theory or model of organizational development. This makes action research possible as it facilitates problem identification, which is essential to determining the proper functioning of an organization. The model suggested here establishes a systematic approach for analyzing relationships among the variables that influence how an organization is managed. The Heart Smart Survey II provides for assessment of three areas of formal and informal activity: moral integrity, a sense of community, and a dedication to service and social justice. The Heart Smart Survey I provides for assessment in ten areas of formal and informal activity (see diagram below). The outer circle in the following table represents an organizational boundary for diagnosis. This boundary demarcates the functioning of the internal and external environments. Since the underlying organizational theory upon which this survey is based is an open-systems model, it is essential that influences from both the internal and external environment be considered for the analysis to be complete.

HEART SMART SCORING SHEET I

Instructions: Transfer the numbers you circled on the questionnaire to the blanks below. Add each column and divide each sum by seven. This will give you comparable scores for each of the ten areas.

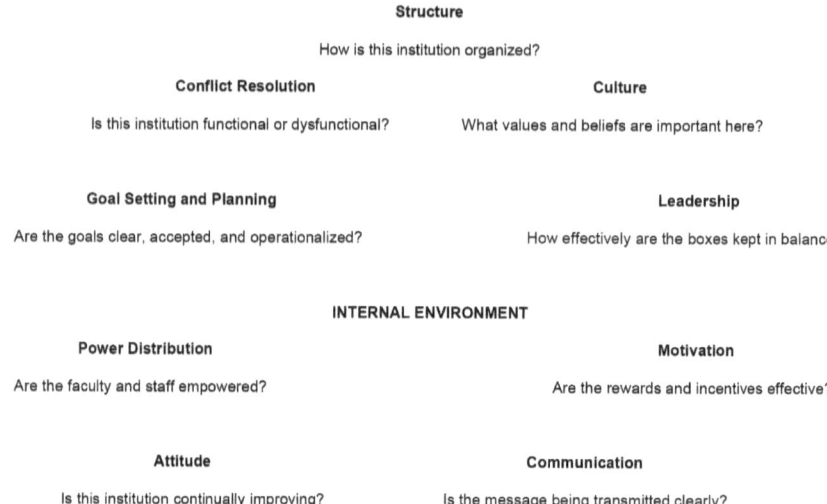

Figure 13.1. The Heart Smart Wheel

Interpretation Sheet (Heart Smart I)

Instructions: Transfer your average scores from the Scoring Sheet to the appropriate boxes in the figure below. Then study the background information and interpretation suggestions that follow.

Background

The Heart Smart Organizational Diagnosis Questionnaire is a survey-feedback instrument designed to collect data on organizational functioning. It measures the perceptions of persons in an organization to determine areas of activity that would benefit from an organizational development effort. It can be used as the sole data-collection technique or in conjunction with other techniques (interview, observation, etc.). The instrument and the model reflect a systematic approach for analyzing relationships among variables that influence how an organization is managed. Using the Heart Smart Organizational Diagnosis Questionnaire is the first step in determining appropriate interventions for organizational change efforts.

Structure	Culture	Leadership	Motivation
1____	2____	3____	4____
11____	12____	13____	14____
21____	22____	23____	24____
31____	32____	33____	34____
41____	42____	43____	44____
51____	52____	53____	54____
61____	62____	63____	64____
Total			

Average _____ _____   _____

Communication	Decision Making	Conflict Resolution	Goal Setting/ Planning
5____	6____	7____	8____
15____	16____	17____	18____
25____	26____	27____	28____
35____	36____	37____	38____
45____	46____	47____	48____
55____	56____	57____	58____
65____	66____	67____	68____
Total			

Average

_____

Power Distribution	Attitude toward Change
9____	10____
19____	20____
29____	30____
39____	40____
49____	50____

Figure 13.2.

Figure 13.3.

Interpretation and Diagnosis

A crucial consideration is the diagnosis based upon data interpretation. The simplest diagnosis would be to assess the amount of variance for each of the ten variables in relation to a score of 4, which is the neutral point. Scores above 4 would indicate a problem with organizational functioning. The closer the score is to 7, the more severe the problem would be. Scores below 4 indicate lack of a problem, with a score of 1 indicating optimum functioning.

Another diagnostic approach follows the same guidelines of assessment in relation to the neutral point (score) of 4. The score of each of the seventy items on the questionnaire can be reviewed to produce more exacting information on problematic areas. Thus, diagnosis would be more precise. For example, let us suppose that the average score on item number 8 is 6.4. This would indicate not only a problem in organizational purpose or goal setting, but also a more specific problem in that there is a gap between organizational and individual goals. This more precise diagnostic effort is likely to lead to a more appropriate intervention in the organization than the generalized diagnostic approach described in the preceding paragraph.

Appropriate diagnosis must address the relationships between the boxes to determine the interconnectedness of problems. For example, if there is a problem with communication, could it be that the organizational structure does not foster effective communication? This might be the case if the average score on item 25 was well below 4 (2.5 or lower) and all the items on organizational structure (1, 11, 21, 31, 41, 51, 61) averaged above 5.5.

Interpretation Sheet (Heart Smart II)

Instructions: Study the background information and interpretation suggestions that follow.

HEART SMART SCORING SHEET II

Instructions: Transfer the numbers you circled on the questionnaire to the blanks below. Add each column and divide each sum by 19. This will give you comparable scores for each of the three areas.

Moral Integrity	Community	Service/Social Justice
1_____	2_____	3_____
4_____	5_____	6_____
7_____	8_____	9_____
10_____	11_____	12_____
13_____	14_____	15_____
16_____	17_____	18_____
19_____	20_____	21_____
22_____	23_____	24_____
25_____	26_____	27_____
28_____	29_____	30_____
31_____	32_____	33_____
34_____	35_____	36_____
37_____	38_____	39_____
40_____	41_____	42_____
43_____	44_____	45_____
46_____	47_____	48_____
49_____	50_____	51_____
52_____	53_____	54_____
55_____	56_____	57_____

Total

_____ _____ _____

Average (Divide by 19)

_____ _____ _____

Average (Divide by 3)

Figure 13.4.

Background

The Heart Smart Organizational Diagnosis Questionnaires are survey-feedback instruments designed to collect data on organizational functioning. They measure the perceptions of persons in an organization to determine areas of activity that would benefit from an organizational development effort. It can be used as the sole data-collection technique or in conjunction with other techniques (interview, observation, and so forth). The instrument and the model reflect a systematic approach for analyzing relationships among variables that influence how an organization is managed. Using the Heart Smart Organizational Diagnosis Questionnaires is the first step in determining appropriate interventions for organizational change efforts.

Interpretation and Diagnosis

A crucial consideration is the diagnosis based upon data interpretation. The simplest diagnosis would be to assess the amount of variance for each of the three variables in relation to a score of 4, which is the neutral point. Scores below 4 would indicate a problem with organizational functioning. The closer the score is to 1, the more severe the problem would be. Scores above 4 indicate lack of a problem, with a score of 7 indicating optimum functioning.

Another diagnostic approach follows the same guidelines of assessment in relation to the neutral point (score) of 4. The score of each of the fifty-seven items on the questionnaire can be reviewed to produce more exacting information on problematic areas. Thus, diagnosis would be more precise. For example, let us suppose that the average score on item number 8 is 2.4. This would indicate not only a problem in the sense of community in the institution, but also a more specific problem in that there are not enough occasions provided for the teachers to interact with one another. This more precise diagnostic effort is likely to lead to a more appropriate intervention in the organization than the generalized diagnostic approach described in the preceding paragraph.

References

Armstrong, K., 1992. *Muhammad: A Biography of the Profit*. San Francisco: Harper.
Baker, W., and O'Malley, M. 2008. *Leading with Kindness*. New York: AMACOM.
Bernstein, C. 1996. *His Holiness*. New York: Penguin.
Biggart, N. W., and Hamilton, G. G. 1987. "An Institutional Theory of Leadership." *Journal of Applied Behavioral Sciences* 23 (4): 429–41.
Bolman, L. G., and Deal, T. E. 1991. *Reframing Organizations: Artistry, Choice, and Leadership*. San Francisco: Jossey-Bass.
Chapple, C. 1993. *The Jesuit Tradition in Education and Missions*. Scranton, PA: University of Scranton Press.
Creel, H. G., 1949. *Confucius: The Man and the Myth*. Westport, CT: Greenwood Press.
De Pree, M. 1989. *Leadership Is an Art*. New York: Dell.
Erickson, F. 1984. "School Literacy, Reasoning and Civility: An Anthropologist's Perspective." *Review of Educational Research* 54.
Ericson, D. P., and Ellett, R. S. 2002. "The Question of the Student in Educational Reform." *Educational Policy Analysis Archives* 10 (31).
Fiedler, R. E., and Garcia, J. E. 1987. *New Approaches to Effective Leadership*. New York: Wiley.
Foster, W. 1986. *Paradigms and Promises*. New York: Prometheus Books.
Glasser, W. 1984. *Control Theory: A New Explanation of How We Control Our Lives*. New York: Harper and Row.
Goleman, D. 1995. *Emotional Intelligence*. New York: Bantam.
Griffiths, D., and Ribbins, P. 1995. "Leadership Matters in Education: Regarding Secondary Headship." Inaugural lecture, University of Birmingham, Edgbaston.
Hersey, P., and Blanchard, K. H. 1969. "Life-Cycle Theory of Leadership." *Training and Development Journal* 23:26–34.
———. 1988. *Management of Organizational Behavior*. Fifth edition. Englewood Cliffs, NJ: Prentice Hall.
Hesse, H. 1951. *Siddhartha*. New York: New Directions.
House, R. J. 1977. "A 1976 Theory of Charismatic Leadership." In J. G. Hunt and Larson, eds., *Leadership: The Cutting Edge*. Carbondale: Southern Illinois University Press.
———. 1999. "How Cultural Factors Affect Leadership." *Global Focus*. July 23. Retrieved from http://knowledge.wharton.upenn.edu.
Ivereigh, A. 2014. *The Great Reformer: Francis and the Making of a Radical Pope*. New York: Henry Holt.

Judge, T. A., and Piccolo, R. F. 2004. "Transformational and Transactional Leadership: A Meta-analytic Test of Their Relative Validity." *Journal of Applied Psychology* 89 (5): 755–68.

Kirkpatrick, S. A., and Locke, E. A. 1991. "Leadership: Do Traits Matter?" *Academy of Management Executive* 5 (2): 48–60.

Liu, W. 1972. *Confucius, His Life and Time*. Westport, CT: Greenwood Press.

Lowney, C. 2003. *Heroic Leadership*. Chicago: Loyola Press.

Loyola, I. 2007. *The Spiritual Exercises of St. Ignatius of Loyola*. New York: Cosimo Classics.

Malherbe, A., and Ferguson, E. 1978. *Gregory of Nyssa: The Life of Moses*. New York: Pauline Press.

Marcello, P. 2006. *Gandhi: A Biography*. Westport, CT: Greenwood Biographies.

Mayer, J. D., Salovey, P., and Caruso, D. R. (2000). Models of Emotional Intelligence. In R. J. Sternberg, ed., *Handbook of Intelligence*, 396–420. Cambridge: Cambridge University Press.

McGregor, D. 1961. *The Human Side of Enterprise*. New York: McGraw Hill.

Northouse, P. G. 2013. *Leadership: Theory and Practice*. Sixth edition. Thousand Oaks, CA: Sage.

Oates, S. 1982. *Let the Trumpet Sound: A Life of Martin Luther King, Jr.* New York: Harper and Row.

Palestini, R. 1999. *Ten Steps to Education Reform: Making Change Happen*. Lanham, MD: Rowman and Littlefield Education.

———. 2011a. *Leadership with a Conscience*. Lanham, MD: Rowman and Littlefield Education.

———. 2011b. *Educational Leadership: Leading with Mind and Heart*. Third edition. Lanham, MD: Rowman and Littlefield Education.

———. 2013. *A Ten-Minute Approach to Educational Leadership*. Lanham, MD: Rowman and Littlefield Education.

———. 2014. *Feminist Theory and Educational Leadership*. Lanham, MD: Rowman and Littlefield Education.

Pastan, A. 2006. *Gandhi*. New York: DK Publishing.

Peters, T., and Waterman, R. 1988. *In Search of Excellence*. New York: Grand Central Publishing.

Ravier, A. 1987. *Ignatius of Loyola and the Founding of the Society of Jesus*. San Francisco: Ignatius Press.

Rook, C., and Agrawal, A. 2013. "Global Leaders East and West—Do All Global Leaders Lead in the Same Way?" *Leadership and Organizations*. http://knowledge.insead.edu/leadership-management.

Senge, P. M. 1990. *The Fifth Dimension: The Art of Practice of the Learning Organization*. New York: Doubleday.

Solzhenitsyn, A. 1978. *A World Split Apart*. New York: Harper and Row.

Spink, K. 1997. *Mother Teresa: An Authorized Biography*. New York: HarperCollins.

Stogdill, R. M., and Coons, A. E., eds. 1957. *Leader Behavior: Its Description and Measurement*. Columbus: Ohio State University Bureau of Business Research.

Toner, J. J. 1991. *Discerning God's Will: Ignatius of Loyola's Teaching on Christian Decision Making*. St. Louis: Institute of Jesuit Sources.

Tripole, M. R. 1994. *Faith Beyond Justice*. St. Louis: Institute of Jesuit Sources.

About the Author

Dr. Robert Palestini is a former graduate dean and currently professor emeritus of educational leadership at Saint Joseph's University in Philadelphia. He is also the founding executive director of the Educational Leadership Institute at SJU. In more than fifty years in education, he has served as a teacher, principal, and superintendent of schools of one of the largest school systems in the United States. He has written more than a dozen books on various aspects of educational leadership.

www.ingramcontent.com/pod-product-compliance
Lightning Source LLC
Chambersburg PA
CBHW030113010526
44116CB00005B/222